CHRIST IN
THE TABERNACLE

—BY—

REV. A. B. SIMPSON, D.D.

————

PUBLISHED BY

CHRISTIAN PUBLICATIONS, Inc.

25 South Tenth Street, Harrisburg, Pa.

The Mark of Vibrant Faith

CONTENTS.

—

CHAPTER I.

The Tabernacle as a Type of Christ.

"And the Lord spake unto Moses, saying Speak unto the children of Israel, that they bring me an offering: of every man that giveth it willingly with his heart ye shall take my offering. And this is the offering which ye shall take of them; gold, and silver, and brass, and blue, and purple, and scarlet, and fine linen, and goats' hair, and rams' skins dyed red, and badgers' skins and shittim wood, oil for the light, spices for anointing oil, and for sweet incense, onyx stones, and stones to be set in the ephod, and in the breastplate. And let them make me a sanctuary; that I may dwell among them. According to all that I shew thee, after the pattern of the tabernacle, and the pattern of all the instruments thereof, even so shall ye make it.

"And they shall make an ark of shittim wood: two cubits and a half shall be the length thereof, and a cubit and a half the breadth thereof, and a cubit and a half the height thereof."—Ex. 25: 1-10.

THE Tabernacle is the grandest of all the Old Testament types of Christ. It was all one great object lesson of spiritual truth. In its wonderful furniture, priesthood, and worship, we see, with a vividness that we find nowhere else, the glory and grace of Jesus, and the privileges of His redeemed peo-

ple. And as in the architect's plan we
can understand the future building better, even, than by looking at the building
without the plan; so, in this pattern
from the mount, we can understand as
nowhere else, that glorious temple of
which Christ is the corner-stone and we
also, as living stones, are built up in Him
a spiritual house, an holy priesthood, to
"offer   sacrifices   acceptable   to   God
through Jesus Christ."

I.

THE FORM AND STRUCTURE OF THE TABER-NACLE.

The Tabernacle was an oblong structure, about forty-five feet long, and fifteen feet wide and high, very similar in
size and proportions to the double par-
lors of an ordinary dwelling-house. It
was constructed of boards and shittim
wood, a peculiarly indestructible materi-
al, overlaid with gold, and fastened with
sockets and tenons of silver. brass, etc.
It was covered with three tiers of skins,
and a fine interior lining of most costly

curtains, embroidered and adorned with symbolical figures, of the highest beauty and spiritual significance. The external covering of the roof was of rough badgers' skins, to protect it from the inclemency of the weather. The exact form of the roof is a matter of dispute, some believing it to have been pitched at an angle, and some an arched or a flat surface.

The Tabernacle itself was divided into two unequal chambers by magnificent curtains called the vail. The inner chamber was a perfect cube, fifteen feet square. It contained the ark of the covenant, over which was the mercy-seat. This was its lid, and consisted of a solid plate of gold. Then, springing from this, and formed of the same piece of solid gold, hovered the cherubim, symbolical figures, representing the faces of the four typical forms of the animate creation—the man, the ox, the eagle, and the lion; while between the meeting wings of the cherubic figures shone the Shekinah, or visible divine glory, a luminous cloud of transcendent brightness, which, perhaps, arose and expanded into the pillar of cloud and fire that hovered above the Tabernacle, and led the march of Israel. This chamber was the Holy of Holies, God's especial presence chamber and throne of grace and glory. None ever entered it except the high priest, and he only once a year.

The other division was twice as large, fifteen feet by thirty, and was called the Holy Place. It was open to the ministering priest only, not to the common people; and it was separated from the outer court by the door, a curtain, also of blue, purple, and scarlet, which none but cleansed and consecrated priests might pass. Its articles of furniture were: the golden candlestick, which was its only light, there being no windows at all; the table of shewbread, covered with twelve loaves crowned with pure frankincense, which were offered to God for one week, and then eaten by the priests, and renewed from Sabbath to Sabbath; and the golden altar of incense, with its accompanying censer, where pure frankincense was continually offered, and from which, once a year on the great Day of Atonement, the high priest with the golden censer took burning coals and smoking incense in his hands, passed through the mysterious vail, entered alone the Holy of Holies, and there made atonement for the people in the immediate presence of God.

Surrounding the Tabernacle was another court, an enclosure eighty-seven by one hundred and seventy-five feet, with an opening on the eastern side, called the gate. Into this court all the people might come.

Two objects of ceremonial worship stood here. Near the gate was the brazen altar of burnt offering. Here the sacrifices of burnt offering were presented, the blood sprinkled, and the fire kept ever burning, from which the altar of incense was supplied. All parts of the Tabernacle had to be sprinkled with blood from this altar. It was the only way of access to the presence of God. Farther in was the brazen laver, a vast basin, perhaps, with polished exterior—forming thus a mirror as well as a foun-

tain,—made from the metal mirrors of
the women of Israel, and so enabling the
priests at once to see their uncleanness
in the metal, and then to wash it away
in the water which it contained. It was
for the purification of the priests as they
entered the sanctuary, and no one could
pass through the door until he had washed in this fountain. The gate of this
enclosure was always open. It had no
hangings as did the two inner doors. All
might freely come into His courts and
bring their offerings for sin and uncleanness.

Outside the gate was the camp of
Israel, forming a square around the
Tabernacle of vast extent, three tribes
on each side, the tribe of Judah being
on the east, opposite the entrance to
the Tabernacle gate. And just beyond,
still farther out, there continually burned
the fire without the camp, where the
bodies of the sin offerings were consumed, and also the refuse of the camp.

Such was this simple and wonderful
structure, God's first sanctuary, and the
type of all that is sacred and precious

in the person and work of Christ, and the privileges of our heavenly calling.

II.

THE ERECTION AND SUBSEQUENT HISTORY OF THE TABERNACLE.

We find two accounts of the construction of the Tabernacle in Exodus. First, we have the Tabernacle as it was planned in heaven, and shown to Moses on the mount as a pattern (Exodus 25: 31). This is the type of Christ set forth from eternity in the counsels of divine love, our Redeemer prepared for us from before the foundation of the world, and revealed in successive types and prophecies, long before His actual incarnation and life on earth. Moses built the Tabernacle according to an actual model which God had shown him during the forty days on the mount. So Christ was born, lived, and died in exact accordance with the prophetic picture of previous ages of revelation.

Then in Exodus (chapters 32 and 33), there is the dark interval of sorrow and

rebellion, during which the people trans-
gressed the covenant they had just entered into, and showed most painfully
the need of the salvation which God had
just been preparing. This is the type
of man's fall, and his failure under the
old dispensation. Christ had been already provided; but man must feel the
need of the divine salvation, by the actual experience of sin. It is touching beyond degree to know, that all the time
that man was rebelling against his God,
God's remedy was waiting in that mount
of grace.

Then, in chapter 34, we come to the
second stage in the history of the Tabernacle, its actual erection according to
the divine plan already shown, and
through the freewill offerings of the people, and the skill and workmanship of
the men whom God had specially endued
for this purpose. Two men were particularly called, and qualified by the gifts of
the Holy Spirit, in sacred art, to origi-
nate and execute all its symbolical decorations, and the women of Israel were
similarly prepared and enabled to make

ready it costly materials. So its entire erection was through the supernatural gifts of the Holy Ghost, as well as the divine plan which was revealed to Moses.

During the forty years of wilderness life, it was borne from place to place in succession by the faithful hands of the Levites, who were appointed for this special ministry. After the entrance into Canaan, it remained for a time at Gilgal, and afterwards was established at Shiloh, which became the religious centre of the national worship for a long time. During the period of the Judges, we lose sight of it for a season, through the subjugation and humiliation of Israel. But we find it afterwards in Nob, in the neighborhood of Jerusalem, in the reign of David. And finally, it was established on Mount Zion through the piety of this good king, where it remained until superseded by the more magnificent Temple of Solomon, which was, however, only a more splendid edition of the same building, containing all the essential features of the Tabernacle, only adding a higher degree of splendor, and so typifying the future glories, as the Tabernacle typifies the grace of Christ and His redemption.

III.

SPIRITUAL AND TYPICAL SIGNIFICANCE OF THE TABERNACLE.

The Tabernacle was designed to represent and prefigure the most important teachings of the Scriptures with reference; first, to Christ; secondly, to the Church; thirdly, to the individual Christian. In these three aspects we shall briefly consider it.

FIRST, AS A TYPE OF CHRIST.

The very word Tabernacle is used with reference to Him in the opening chapter of the Gospel of John, fourteenth verse. "The Word was made flesh, and tabernacled among us (and we beheld his glory, the glory as of the only begotten of the Father), full of grace and truth."

Again, in the ninth chapter of Hebrews, the apostle after describing the structure of the ancient sanctuary, applies it all to the person and work of Christ.

The points of comparison are almost unlimited. Among them may be mentioned:

(a). The location of the Tabernacle, which was entered from the camp of Judah, suggests the fact that Christ was born of the tribe of Judah.

(b). The materials of which the Tabernacle was constructed; namely, indestructible wood and pure gold, suggest His perfect humanity on the one hand, and His supreme Divinity on the other.

(c). The colors which were so constantly mingled in the Tabernacle, especially the prevailing hues of white, blue, scarlet, and purple, all point to qualities in Him; the white, His spotless purity; the blue, His heavenly origin; the scarlet, His sufferings and death; the purple, His kingly glory.

(d). The external plainness in contrast with the internal glory of the Tabernacle: the badgers' skins without, and the gold and Shekinah glory within, proclaim the lowliness of Christ's earthly

state, and yet the beauty and glory of
His character and inner presence, as He
reveals Himself to the soul that abides
in Him.

(*e*). The contrast between the Tabernacle and the temple, the one a shifting
tent, exposed to constant vicissitude and
humiliation, the other combining in itself all the glory of earth and heaven,
suggests to us, the earthly life of our
Lord and His exaltation and the kingly
glory of His millennial reign.

(*f*). The fact that the Tabernacle was
the place of God's manifestation of Himself to Israel, and the place where He
revealed the symbols of His immediate
presence, reminds us of Him who is Himself the image and manifestation of God,
and whose very name, "Emmanuel,"
means "God with us."

(*g*). The Tabernacle was God's meet-
ing-place with Israel. "There will I
meet with them from between the cherubim," were His own words; "and there
they heard the voice of God speaking
from between the cherubim." And so
the Lord Jesus Christ is the only way

of access to the Father, and my fellowship with heaven. "If a man love me,
my father will love him, and we will
come to him and make our abode with
him."

(*h*). The Tabernacle was the place of
sacrifice. Its most vivid spectacle was
the flowing and the sprinkled blood, and
it tells us in every part of the sacrifice
of Christ.

(i). Not only was it the place of sacrifice, but also the place of cleansing; the
blood atoned and the water washed away
the stain of defilement. So "Christ is
the fountain for sin and for uncleanness." He gave Himself for the
Church, that He might sanctify and
cleanse it by the washing of water by
the Word, and purify unto Himself a
glorious Church not having spot nor
wrinkle.

(j). The Tabernacle was the place
where the guilty might freely come to
the altar of atonement. And Jesus Christ
is the propitiation not only for our sins,
but also for the sins of the whole world.

(*k*). The Tabernacle had inner cham-

2

bers. And so it speaks of the deeper life, and the fuller blessings into which those may enter who are willing to abide in Christ. "I am the door," He says, "and I am come that they might have life, and that they might have it more abundantly." He is our life, our bread, our light, our altar of prayer, our open vail of access even to the innermost presence of the holy God.

(*l*). The Tabernacle was the place where the law was enshrined in the bosom of the ark, and ever covered by the sprinkled blood which proclaimed the sinner's acceptance. So Jesus keeps for us the divine law, then keeps it also in us, by His indwelling life and presence, and so becomes our perfect righteousness.

(*m*). The cherubim of glory in the Holy of Holies were types of Christ's exalted glory, of His humanity crowned with the strength of the ox, the majesty of the lion, and the loftiness of the eagle's flight. All this He is as the pledge of our future glory.

All this and much more we see in this

ancient object lesson concerning Him of whom Moses and the prophets did write, and which He came Himself to fulfill, with a fullness which He will yet enable us more fully to understand in every detail respecting this pattern in the mount.

SECONDLY: THE TABERNACLE AS A TYPE OF THE CHURCH.

That which is true of Christ the Head, is also true of His body, the Church. Among other points of instruction which the Tabernacle suggests in this connection, it may be noticed:

(a). Like the Tabernacle, the Church has been planned by God Himself, and is in no sense a human institution. It should in every respect be organized, constituted, built up, and equipped according to the pattern which Christ has shown us Himself, "Teaching them to observe all things, whatsoever I have commanded."

(b). The Church requires the same divine anointing through the Holy Ghost, on the part of all who, like Bezaleel and Aholiab, are engaged in her spiritual upbuilding, not the gifts of intellect-

ual brilliancy, but the wisdom of the
Holy Ghost, and the enduement of His
power. These alone can accomplish de-
finite and eternal results and all else will
wither and drift away in the fiery blasts
of the great ordeal.

(c). The Church, like the ancient Tabernacle, should have her chief beauty
within, not in costly decorations, but in
the glory of the indwelling God and the
exhibition of a crucified and sin-cleans-
ing Saviour. Without this, she can only
be what Israel's temple was when the
Master and the Shekinah departed, and
the avengers came with fire and blood.
Without this His word can only be,
"Your house is left unto you desolate,"
or, as it was the Church of the Lao-
diceans, because they were neither cold
nor hot, "I will spue thee out of my
mouth."

(d). Like the ancient Tabernacle, the
Church should have her inner chambers
for deeper teaching and closer fellowship, in the Holy Place, in the light of
the sevenfold lamp of truth, and at the
table of the heavenly bread; while the

sweet fragrance from the golden altar
fills all the place with the breath of heav-
en, and the rent vail just beyond reveals
and opens up to her vision even the innermost chambers of heaven itself, from
which ever shines the Shekinah of His
abiding presence.

(e). Like the ancient Tabernacle, the
Church should be the repository of the
world's true light and living bread, the
light of the world, and the steward of
the mysteries of God.

(f). Like the ancient Tabernacle and
temple, the Church has her earthly and
her heavenly life, the time of desert wan-
dering and vicissitude, but the prospect
also of a glory greater than that of Solomon's temple, when the Lamb shall
gather His redeemed on Mount Zion, and
the universe shall come to gaze on the
glories of the New Jerusalem, prepared
as a bride adorned for her husband.

THIRDLY: THE TABERNACLE AS THE TYPE OF CHRISTIAN LIFE.

What is true of Christ, is true in the
individual measure of each one of His

people. "As he is, so are we also in this world." Let us not fear, therefore, to claim the fullness of our great salvation.

CONDEMNATION.

The first chapter in every Christian's existence is the dark, sad chapter of condemnation. This was vividly set forth in the ancient camp of Israel, by the fire that ever burned without the camp, suggesting the wrath of God revealed from heaven against all unrighteousness of men. That fire consumed the offering to which sin had been transferred, and it must likewise consume all whose sins are not transferred to that burnt offering. If He, in the place of the sinner, suffered this vengeance, how shall we escape if we dare to stand before God covered with our guilt and corruption? "If they do these things in a green tree, what shall be done in the dry?" Our Lord has not quenched this fire, but left it still burning outside the gate of the Gospel for all that reject Him. "He that believeth not, is condemned already." "He that believeth not the Son shall not see life; but the wrath of God abideth on him.''

SALVATION.

The next stage in the believer's life is salvation. We now enter the gate and stand within the court. We may freely come. There is no barrier, not even a fold of a curtain intervening. We hasten through the inviting entrance, and stand before the smoking altar which tells us of the Cross and the blood through which we have redemption from sin. We place our hand upon the head of the sacrifice, and we become partakers of the great expiation.

Next, the laver speaks to us of the Holy Ghost, whose power regenerates and cleanses the soul from sin; and we wash in its fountain, and are qualified and authorized to enter into the inner presence, and into the more intimate fellowship of the Holy Place.

CONSECRATION, COMMUNION.

The Tabernacle also tells us of the next stage of Christian experience and life—communion, consecration, sanctification, and abiding fellowship with Christ. That inner chamber just beyond the open court is only for God's priests. How, then, may we dare to intrude? Thank God, we are all admitted to the place of priesthood, if we will accept by "him that loved us, and washed us from our sins in his own blood. And hath made us kings and priests unto God." Not a few, now, but "all are a royal priesthood, a holy nation, a peculiar people." So we may boldly enter in, but not until we have washed in that cleansing laver, as well as sacrificed at the altar. We must accept His sanctifying as well as justifying grace. Even to Peter, who had been bathed, that is, justified, Christ said, "If I wash thee not, thou hast no part with me." Although we have boldness by the blood of Jesus even to enter into the Holiest, yet we must come with "hearts sprinkled from an evil conscience, and our bodies washed with pure water." Thus divinely cleansed, "let us draw near with a true heart, in full assurance of faith."

Our great High Priest is standing within, and sweetly saying, "I am the door; by me if any man enter in, he shall be saved, and go in and out, and find pasture."

What pasture! There is the sevenfold lamp which speaks of Christ and the Holy Spirit, our perfect light; the light of truth; the light which reveals Himself; the light of heavenly vision; the light which brings sight as well as light to our dull eyes; the light of guidance and direction amid the perplexities of life and His own continual presence and voice as the shepherd, as well as the door; and the light which will shine through us and from us as the light of men.

The living bread! The table with its twelve loaves, one for each of us, made from the finest of the wheat, ever renewed with each returning Sabbath! Not only bread, but frankincense like honey out of the rock, all the sweetness of his consolations, as well as the strength of his life! Bread that nourishes both soul and body, and becomes our perfect life

and sustenance! Then not only is there
the bread, but all that is implied in the
altar of incense. This includes all that
is involved in a life of prayer and communion with God through Jesus Christ.
That incense, together with the anointing oil, was the most sacred thing in all
the Tabernacle service. It might not
be imitated by mortal art, but was consecrated sacredly for the service of God
alone. It was compounded of many ingredients and some of it, we are told,
was beaten very small, and then was
burned with sweet spices on that pure
altar (Ex. 30: 33-34).

So the spirit of prayer must be
born from above, and cannot be imitated nor counterfeited by merely human effort. It springs from the com-
bination of all the circumstances of
life and qualites of our Christian character. It is the flower of piety, and the
fragrance of the heart, distilled like perfume, indescribably delicate, pure and
heavenly. Nothing is too small to enter
into it, and become an occasion for it.
The incense of prayer may be beaten

very small, and rise from a thousand tri-
fles in our life which we may so consecrate to God as to become a sacrifice of
a sweet smelling savor. Our little trials
and trifling ministries, laid on this golden
altar, become to Him like the fragrance
of the spring, and the breath of Aaron's
censer; and He treasures them in heav-
en in "vials full of odors, which are the
prayers of saints." But in order to be
divinely fragrant, they must be set on
fire by the Holy Ghost, the true Interces-
sor and Advocate on earth, as Christ is
the Advocate on high, making intercession "within us with groanings which
cannot be uttered."

The sweet incense of the Holy Place
penetrated through the vail, and filled
the Holy of Holies. And so the spirit of
prayer makes both earth and heaven one.
The altar stood at the very entrance to
the inner chamber, and so when we are
rapt in fellowship with God, we are
at the gate of heaven and almost
within the vail. We can hear the voices
and catch the breath from those inner
chambers. Happy are they who thus

abide in Him, in the atmosphere of ceaseless communion and peace! The most
trying place will be fragrant, like odors
of heaven, and the most lonely spot a
little sanctuary where all heaven will
seem to be around us with its Almighty
protection, its blessed companionship,
and its unspeakable joy.

GLORY.

The innermost chamber in the Hebrew
Tabernacle was the Holy of Holies. It
speaks to us of heaven itself, the immediate presence of God, and the glory
which awaits us at His coming or our
translation within the gates. It tells us
of a heaven not far off, shut out of our
vision, but near and open. The vail is
rent in twain from top to bottom, and
the Holy of Holies sheds its light and
glory all around us, even here; so that
translation itself is scarcely a change of
companionship, although it may be of
location. That inner chamber tells us
of the place where our prayers can enter
now in sweet incense, and be accepted
in His name. Our eyes can look through
the vail, and see heaven open, and Jesus

standing on the right hand of God. There the sprinkled blood on the mercy-seat is ever pleading for us, and claiming our perfect and perpetual acceptance. There the ark within the vail, with the unbroken law within its bosom, is the symbol of the perfect righteousness which we share with Him, and in which we stand accepted in Him, even in the immediate presence of God. There the cherubim of glory are the patterns of the dignity and royalty which our redeemed humanity has already attained in Christ, its illustrious Head, and which we shall share in its fullness when He shall appear. As we look through, we know that our spirits, too, shall follow, and be with Him where He is. "The feet that tremble and falter shall walk through the gates of day;" and the very body of our humiliation shall be like him, when he shall appear, and shall be changed into the image of "the body of his glory."

And all this we have even here, not only in vision and prospect, but in fore-taste.

"The holy to the holiest leads,
　To this our spirits rise,
And he who in His footsteps treads,
　Shall meet Him in the skies."

IV.

THE ANOINTING OF THE TABERNACLE.

After the Tabernacle had been fully completed, according to all the patterns shown in the mount, it was solemnly dedicated to God, and the entire tent and its furniture were anointed with oil, specially prepared according to the divine prescription, and consecrated to this exclusive purpose, and then the manifestation of the divine presence appeared upon it. The pillar of cloud spread its curtains above it, and the Shekinah glory took its place between the cherubim, and filled the tent so completely, that Moses, even, was not able to enter the Holy Place. Moses had simply and perfectly obeyed God's directions, and now God accepted his work, and put His seal upon it. This was symbolical of the anointing of Jesus Christ with the Holy Ghost, and of the same anointing which comes upon every consecrated heart when it has obeyed the divine directions, and presented itself a living sacrifice to God. God will so fill such a soul, that there shall be no room for self and sin. This, indeed, is the true secret of sanctification and self-crucifixion; the expulsive power of the Holy Ghost and the divine presence are the only true antidotes to the power of self and Satan.

Henceforth, the Tabernacle becomes the seat and centre of the divine manifestation. We thus observe three stages of the manifested presence of God in Exodus; namely, the pillar of cloud and fire that went before; the presence from the mount; and now, the presence of Jehovah in the Tabernacle. We trace the same three stages in the Old Testament: first, the spirit of God as manifested in the patriarchial dispensation; secondly, the revelation of God under the law; and thirdly, the revelation of God in Christ, the True Tabernacle. "God, who at sundry times and in divers manners spake in times past unto the fathers by the prophets, hath in these last days

spoken unto us by his Son, whom he
hath appointed heir of all things, by
whom also he made the worlds''; Hence
we find God in the very first verse of
Leviticus, speaking to Moses no longer
out of the mount or cloud, but out of the
Tabernacle. So we may find in Christ
the continual presence and guidance of
our covenant God. ''If a man love me,''
Christ says, ''he will keep my sayings,
and my Father will love him, and we
will come unto him and make our abode
with him.'' Let us only do what Moses
did, yield ourselves fully and implicity
to the divine will, hand ourselves over
as the property of Christ, and we shall
also be possessed and filled with a glory
as divine as the Shekinah, and as endur-
ing as the life and love of God.

Henceforth this event, the setting up
and anointing of the Tabernacle, becomes
a landmark of time. It was to begin the
second year of their national history, and
was on the first day of the first month.
The first year had begun with the Pass-
over, but this forms the next great era
of their existence.

And so the moment when the soul is dedicated and anointed by the Holy Ghost is an eternal era in its history, as important as the hour of its new birth, the beginning of months and years, from which all its experiences and hopes are henceforth measured. Have we entered upon this second year? Have we begun it, like them, with the sacrifice of our being in implicit obedience, on the altar of God?

And have we received the descending fire, and the abiding Comforter, henceforth to speak to us, not from the heavens, nor even from the tables of stone, but from the inner chambers of His sanctuary in our hearts?

CHAPTER II.

The Altar and the Blood.

"And thou shalt make an altar of shittim wood, five cubits long and five cubits broad; the altar shall be foursquare; and the height thereof shall be three cubits," etc. "For the life of the flesh is in the blood: and I have given it to you upon the altar, to make atonement for your souls: for it is the blood that maketh an atonement for the soul." "Forasmuch as ye know that ye were not redeemed with corruptible things, as silver and gold, from your vain conversation received by tradition from your fathers; but with the precious blood of Christ, as of a lamb without blemish and without spot."— Ex. 27: 1; Lev. 17: 11; 1. Pet. 1: 18.

THIS is a brief description of the altar of burnt offering in the ancient Tabernacle. It was the first object that you would notice as you entered the court of that ancient sanctuary, standing just inside, and accessible to all the people. It was a large frame of wood, covered with brass, sufficient to hold any offering that might be placed upon it. There was a fire constantly burning upon it and the sacrifice was renewed every day, ever burning, ever smoking, ever blood-stained, ever open to any guilty Hebrew that might want to approach it.

It was so connected with the interior of the Tabernacle that everyone that went in had to pass it, and had to take the blood from its sacrifices, in order to be accepted in the Holy Place. Everything in that Holy Place was sprinkled with the blood, and the very high priest, when he entered the innermost shrine, must bring that blood, or he would be smitten with death. Thus it had a very important part in the worship of the sanctuary.

1. Its place at the entrance of the Tabernacle teaches us that Christ's sacrifice, of which it is the type, stands at the very entrance of all our access to and communion with God.

2. Then again, the relation which it bore to the inner sections of the sanctuary, and to the fact that its blood was necessary in order to enter the inner shrine, shows us that Christ's blood is the only passport now to the presence of God, either in earth or in heaven;

and that, with it, we are accepted either
on earth or in heaven, to the very presence of God.

3. It was accessible to the highest and
the lowest, to every class of people. This
indicates the fullness and graciousness of
the great atonement which Christ has
made for the sins of the whole world, sufficient for all, though effectual only for
those that believe.

These are the chief lessons of the altar. We might add that there was
nothing ornamental about it; it was rude,
and unpretentious, and ghastly looking;
it was made of brass, to bear the heaviest
burdens, and to sustain the streams of
gore that bathed it, and the ceaseless
fires that burned upon it.

It was a place of suffering, and blood,
and it bore the constant mark of sin.
So the Cross of Calvary, the death of
Christ, and the whole doctrine of the
atonement, have nothing very sentimen-
tal about them. The culture of man does
not like it; the philosophy of the world
would get rid of it if it could. But God
has made His people prize the precious

blood of Jesus Christ above all price and
honor and love.

But passing on from this interesting
object, let us fix our attention on that
of which this altar was the most em-
phatic expression, THE BLOOD, that emblem that runs not only through the
Tabernacle and the altar, but which we
find in all the types. We shall speak of
seven places in which we find the blood
particularly emphasized.

I. First, we find the blood on the door
posts of the houses of the children of
Israel. We find it sprinkling the lintels on
that night when they escaped death by
the destroying angel's wing; the blood
kept them safe. This may stand, then, for
redeeming blood. Your life was forfeited
to death, but He redeemed you and put
His mark of purchase above your head.
"Worthy is the Lamb that was slain to
receive power, and riches, and wisdom,
and strength, and honor, and glory, and
blessing." He has redeemed us; He has
bought me personally, and you personally. When I bring it home to my heart,
it melts and breaks my heart to pieces

to remember that He saw me in my ruin
and took me and my responsibilities,
suffered for me, loved me individually
and by His very blood bought me back
from the bondage and penalty of sin.

II. Secondly, we see this blood on the
altar. It is spilt blood, shed blood; it is
blood drunk in by the earth; it is the
blood of atonement. The blood on the
door is redeeming blood. The blood on
the altar is atoning blood. By that I mean
blood that washes out your guilt, blood
that pays your penalty, blood that meets
your obligations, death instead of your
death, a life given instead of my life
and yours. It has the significance of
expiation and propitiation. Christ is the
propitiation for our sins. He has borne
our penalty for sin, and we are free.

III. In the third place, we see the
blood on the leper. We find, especially
in Leviticus 14, the picture of the leper,
that hideous object of uncleanness and
type of sin. We see him brought to the
priest; we see the blood sprinkled upon
him; we see the blood of the little bird
touching his ear, his hand, and his foot,

in token that he is cleansed by the blood.
We therefore have redeeming, atoning,
and cleansing blood. "The blood of
Jesus Christ cleanses us from all sin."
It heals from spiritual leprosy; it washes
out our stains; it puts new life into our
being, excluding the old, just as the new
leaves of the spring push off the old
leaves of the autumn. Just as the new
blood in the body throws off the old
mortifying flesh, and heals the wound,
and makes it slough off the corruption
and disease, so the blood of Jesus Christ
cleanses us from sin, and keeps us clean.
Dear friends, is it keeping you? This
subject is nothing, if it is merely a theory
or a thought. It is everything, it is our
life. Can you say

> "O the blood, the precious blood,
> Which Jesus shed for me,
> Upon the Cross a cleansing flood,
> Just now by faith I see!"

IV. Again, we see the blood upon the
book of the covenant. We are told in
the book of Leviticus that Moses was to
take the Book of the Law and bring it
before the people; he was to sprinkle

the blood over the Book, and the very
commandments were to be touched with
the drops, which were the types of Jesus'
blood. What is that? Why, it is the
covenant blood; it seals the covenant;
it pledges the promises; it answers for
our failures; it guarantees our blessings.
The blood of Jesus is on your Bible, on
the commandments, on all your promises.
O beloved, there is not a promise in this
Bible that you claim but the blood of
Jesus Christ has touched it, endorsed
it, purchased it for you.

V. Again, we find the blood on the
priests, and vessels of the sanctuary.
They were dedicated to God by blood.
The right thumb, right ear, and right
toe of the priests were touched with the
blood. So the blood consecrates us, as
well as atones for and redeems us; as
it set apart the Tabernacle and the priest,
it sets apart you and me. We dare not
claim to be our own. If we dared, our
very sense of honesty would make us
blush to live for ourselves, and then to
look up to heaven and say, ''You have
redeemed me, dear Father, and now I am

going to do just as I have a mind to.''
The very consciousness that you have
been redeemed from death, makes you
realize that everything you are, or have,
belongs to Christ. "Ye are not your
own; ye are bought with a price." So
bring your right ear and consecrate it
to hear only for God, your right thumb
to work only for God, and your right
foot, that it may walk only where Christ
has walked before.

VI. Again, we find the blood on the
mercy-seat, within the sacred curtains on
that golden lid, in the Holy of Holies,
under the flashing wings of the cherubim,
and the Shekinah glory; there was the
blood in the most sacred place of all.

The high priest carried it on the Day
of Atonement and sprinkled it there before God's very eye, on the mercy-seat,
where it constantly remained pleading
for the people, standing as the type of
Christ's precious life. For the blood is
the life which He not only laid down on
earth, but which He took up and carried
into heaven, and which He offers there
at God's feet. He has presented it to

God as the price and gift of redeemed
man, and it pleads evermore for us before the throne. So the heavens are
dedicated with blood as well as the earth,
and this moment, Jesus' blood is speaking there for you just as forcibly as on
earth eighteen hundred years ago. So
this might be expressed as *the pleading
blood*. It is Christ's life; it is Christ's
death; it is Christ's great love; it is
Christ's merits pleading for us evermore, and claiming for us that we can
claim according to His will.

During the Franco-Prussian war, in
one of the regiments where discipline
was very strict, one of the soldiers had
disobeyed orders and was to be shot under sentence of court martial. He was in
great agony of mind and, as the hour
approached for the execution, the chaplain was sent to him. He tried to talk
with him. He said, "Are you ready to
die?" "No," replied the prisoner, "I
am not ready, but that does not trouble
me. I am so troubled about my wife
and little children, thinking of their sorrow, and of their future, and such a

memory as they will have of me, and thinking of the years of misery and sorrow they will have to go through, I cannot even think of my soul. Oh, I am so distressed! I am in despair!" There was a fine fellow in the regiment who heard all this, a Christian man, well advanced in years. He was greatly affected, and stepping forward, he said, "I will tell you what I will do. I have no wife nor children to mourn for me: it will be nothing to me to die; I would be glad to be with my Lord; let me die in your place." He talked to the chaplain and the commanding officer. They were greatly affected, but they did not know what to do, and they referred it to the superior officer. He could hardly believe it; he said, "Do you really mean it?" "Yes," he said, "there can be no question about it; that poor fellow is not ready to die; it would be eternal death to him. To me it would be but a quick translation to Him to whom I am going soon; I have not a friend on earth who would be the worse for it. I am ready to go. Let me take his place."

They were greatly touched and perplexed, and said, "We never had anything like this; we have no authority to make such a substitution. Suppose we defer the case for a day or two, to lay it before the Crown Prince." So they galloped off to the Crown Prince, the man following, and brought the case before this man, one of the noblemen of the century. He was deeply moved. "My brave fellow," he said, "I have no authority to take the life of an innocent man. But I have the power to pardon, and for your sake I will pardon this man. I will take your life as though it had been given for his. Go back and tell him." What a light it sheds on this scene! There was One who had a right to shed His blood, and whose life has been given. And now His blood pleads for us. It is that noble life that pleads for a sinner. And so Christ, the admiration of every angel, of every saint, of the Father Eternal, went down and walked through the world that the law might be honored, that He might show this wretched race that some one could keep

the commandments. Now He pleads by
His merits for us unworthy sinful men.
And so He is represented in the book
of Revelation, as silently standing "as
a Lamb that has been slain." That is
why no promise is too hard to claim.
That is why faith can take all things in
His name.

VII. The living blood.   Let us read
some of Christ's words about it. "Whosoever drinketh my blood, hath eternal
life; and I will raise him up at the last
day. He that drinketh my blood, dwelleth in me and I in him." The blood of
Christ is His life. It is the life of our
soul; it is the life of our body. It is
not merely the death of Jesus for us,
but it is the fact even today, that Jesus
has fresh life to impart to us every
moment, just as in medical science, sometimes, they take the blood from one person's veins, and transfuse it into another's veins and the patient receives
new strength and life. In Germany, before the death of the late German Emperor, a peasant offered him his larynx.
He said, "You can have my windpipe,

my throat, my noble emperor." The
surgeons considered it gravely, and were
greatly moved at his offer to sacrifice
his life. They said, "Poor fellow, it
would not be of any use; it would not be
a living organ." Thanks to His name,
He can put His living organs into us;
He can put His living blood into us.
Blood is not anything unless quickened
by life. Pour that blood into a vessel,
and it is putrid in a few hours, but pour
it into your veins, and it is a magnetic
force throbbing with life. "The life is
in the blood." That is the reason that
Christ makes so much of the blood. Oh,
for the sacred flow, pouring His life more
perfectly and constantly and fully into
our weary souls, into our cold affections,
into our weak purposes, into our weary
nerves! I know there is quickening in
Him, but I also know that it must be
constantly claimed and kept, by habitual
trust and communion.

So this living, quickening blood is the
life of our whole being. So have we
seen the blood on the door, which is redeeming blood; the blood on the altar,

which is atoning blood; the blood on
the leper, which is cleansing blood; the
blood on the book, which is covenant
blood; the blood on the priest, which is
consecrating blood; the blood on the
mercy seat, which is pleading blood; and,
finally, the quickening blood giving life
to the soul and body and keeping us
alive and strengthened through the life
which comes from His heart. May we
echo back the words, "The precious
blood of Christ!" Lord, teach us more
to know its sacred meaning and say,
"Thy blood is drink indeed."

CHAPTER III.

THE WATER.

"And the Lord spake unto Moses saying, Thou shalt also make a laver of brass, and his foot also of brass, to wash withal; and thou shalt put it between the tabernacle of the congregation and the altar, and thou shalt put water therein; for Aaron and his sons shall wash their hands and feet thereat. When they go into the tabernacle of the congregation, they shall wash with water, that they die not; or when they come near to the altar to minister, to burn offering made by fire unto the Lord; so they shall wash their hands and their feet, that they die not: and it shall be a statute forever to them, even to him and to his seed throughout their generations."—Exod. 30: 17-21. "Jesus answered him, if I wash thee not, thou hast no part with me. Simon Peter said unto him, Lord, not my feet only, but also my hands and my head. Jesus saith to him, He that is washed needeth not save to wash his feet, but is clean every whit: and ye are clean, but not all."—John 13: 8-10.

THE figure of water is universally familiar, and represents one of the most important and necessary elements in the physical universe. We find it in the vast ocean, comprising by far the largest part of the earth's surface, and in our iniand lakes and rivers, which form such exquisite networks, both of beauty and convenience and of commercial value, throughout both continents. We find it in the vapor of the skies and the dews that gather about the vegetable creation, preserving it from withering through our torrid summer. We find it forming the largest proportionate part of our own bodies, and everything we call solid and substantial in the world. It is a figure of purity and refreshing, of quickening life and power, of vastness and of abundance. Without it, life could not be for a single moment maintained.

And so we find it in the Bible as one of the most important symbols of spiritual things. Away back in Eden, there were four rivers which watered the garden and were, without doubt, types of the grace with which mankind was to be supplied. We find it again in the preservation of the life of Hagar and her son, supplied by the angelic agency. We find Moses striking it from the rock for the children of Israel, and we see them gathering around it with songs of joy and gladness, and it becomes the

4

source of supply in all their wanderings.
It appears in the ministry of Elisha and
Elijah. It brings healing to Naaman and
saves Jehoshaphat's army from destruc-
tion. In Ezekiel's vision we have the
fountain of water where the filthy wash
and become clean from their idolatries
and the vices which flow from the temple
of vision. Zechariah tells us of a fountain
open for sin and uncleanness. When we
come to the New Testament, John's bap-
tism was the symbol by which the Lord's
reign was ushered in, and Christ carries
the figure farther to imply not only
repentance but, also, regeneration and
sanctification. "Except a man be
born of water and of the Spirit, he cannot enter the kingdom of God." In His
talk with the woman of Samaria, He gave
it an exquisite expression. In the service of the Feast of Tabernacles, He used
the vessels with which men poured out
the water, as symbols of the water which
He would give, even the rivers of waters
which He says shall flow forth from them
that believe. From His own pierced body
comes forth a stream of blood and water

for the healing of the nations. The epistles of the New Testament are filled with the figure of water. Again and again we read of the cleansing and the purity which He comes to bring to the world. And in the Apocalypse it appears in the vision of the finished work of redemption, and the river of the water of life. The whole volume closes with this exquisite passage that points back to all the preceding figures, "Let him that is athirst come; and whosoever will, let him take of the water of life freely."

And so this laver, of which we have read a description, stands just in the centre of one of the most far-reaching of all the figures of the Holy Scriptures. In the Tabernacle, and the whole Levitical ceremony there were various uses made of water. The priesthood had to be set apart by cleansing. The leper had to wash himself with water and be shaved and sprinkled with blood and anointed with oil. They had also the water of separation with which those who had touched the dead had to be cleansed before entering the Tabernacle.

This laver, or basin, was the second article of furniture in the Tabernacle. It was formed out of the brazen mirrors of the women of Israel, which they had brought from the land of Egypt, perhaps with excusable vanity, and perhaps without realizing that these belonged to their old life. When the Lord got them into the wilderness, He gently drew from them these memorials of their old life and consecrated them to a higher purpose, as he did the materials from which they made this brazen laver. They were first melted, and then cast into this basin. It was, perhaps, four or five feet high, and there were a number of faucets opening below the basin and falling into a receptacle. We read of the laver with his foot; no doubt below there were basins into which the waste water could fall.

It consisted of three parts really. First, it was a mirror itself, polished so finely the priests could see their faces in the brazen exterior, a looking-glass, in which they could see, not their beauty, but their blemishes. Then it was a fountain of water for their cleansing, and

further it had receptacles or basins at
the foot where they could come and be
cleansed when they saw their defilement.

The position of this laver was just beyond the altar of offering; it was to be
used by the priests alone, and it was to
be used always by them before entering
the Holy Place. They were not permitted
to go into God's presence with a spot
or stain upon them. They had to do this
before they could go in and offer their
service. Neither could they go to the
brazen altar which stood outside, with
their offerings, until they had washed in
this laver.

Now you have the picture of the laver,
let us gather the lessons.

1. The materials out of which it was
made, and its use as a mirror reflecting
the defilement upon the garment of the
priests, suggest our first lesson; that is,
that God has provided for us in His word
and Spirit the influences by which we are
to discover our own uncleanness and defilement, and we must never forget that
this is a very large part of the functions
of the Spirit. All Scripture is given

for doctrine (that is, teaching), but also
"for reproof, for correction, for instruction in righteousness, that the man
of God may be perfect, thoroughly fur-
nished unto all good works." God expects
us to go to Him that He may reveal our
shortcomings and blemishes and we
should be glad to see them even by painful methods.   The Holy Ghost is the
gentle reprover, quickly giving us the
sense of evil; as if by the sense of smell,
the soul will have the instinctive sensi-
bility to sin, quickly throwing it off and
applying the blood of Jesus Christ to
cleanse from its very shadow. Now, dear
friends, let us take God's mirror to show
us where we fail.   Let us not be so en-
cased in the idea of being infallible and
unreprovable, that we shall fail to get
these lessons.   Let us be glad, not that
we made a mistake, but that that mistake
has shown us something in which we
are yet to be made stronger, as it shall be
overcome.   Let us thank God for this
polished mirror, and say as the Psalmist
said, "Cleanse thou me from secret
faults. Keep back thy servant also from

presumptuous sins; let them not have dominion over me.''

Don't turn away from the Bible because it throws a reproving light on your soul. Don't shrink from prayer because it gives you a sense of an unworthiness and guilt but remember that the laver, which shows the sin, is the fountain which will also wash it away.

2. Again, turn from this view of the laver as a mirror, to look at it as the fountain of cleansing. Water, in the Scriptures, is the chief symbol of the Holy Spirit. Blood tells us of the lamb; water tells us of the dove. God has sent one special person, and His business is to make us clean, to purify and keep us spotless as His own unsullied wing. To this work God has given a divine person, the infinite and Almighty Spirit, one filled with all possible resources for this work. Remember it is His business; you are not imposing upon Him when you bring your uncleanliness. He has been sent, commissioned thus to fulfill the blessed redemption work of our Saviour Jesus Christ. How precious it is to

know that this Person is not away up
in the heavens, but is present in your
heart, ready to stoop down to your uncleanliness and enter your foul heart, and
stay there until there is not a spot, even
as Jesus stooped at the feet of Peter,
and washed those feet with His own
hands. Dear friends, the Holy Ghost is
God's purifying messenger to you, bringing the water and the fire that will make
us white as snow. Let us trust Him; let
us obey Him; let us receive Him; and
let us feel that we shall be without ex-
cuse for our failures if we do not.

Again, the figure of water stands not
only for the Holy Ghost, but for the
Word of God, through which usually the
Spirit of God works. We find it employed
not only to denote the Holy Ghost,
but the Word: "That he might cleanse
the church by the washing of water by
the word." "Now ye are clean through
the word which I have spoken unto you."
Christ's word is the cleansing stream of
the Spirit. "Sanctify them through
truth; thy word is truth." It first shows
us our impurity, God's law, Christ's com-

mandments. The sermon on the mount,
the thousand directions of Christian
duty show us where ye come short; they
show the path of purity. But that is not
the best, they give the promise of cleansing by which we are enabled to receive
and retain His sanctifying grace. And
so we read: ''Having therefore these
promises, dearly beloved, let us cleanse
ourselves from all filthiness of the flesh
and spirit, perfecting holiness in the fear
of God.'' And so Peter says in his second epistle: ''Whereby are given to us
exceeding great and precious promises;
that by these ye might be partakers of
the divine nature, having escaped the
corruption that is in the world through
lust.'' Do you find any lack of purity?
Take His promise and claim it. What
can you want more than this? ''If any
man sin, we have an advocate with the
Father, Jesus Christ the Righteous.''
There is the remedy for any defilement.
''If we confess our sins, he is faithful
and just to forgive us our sins, and
cleanse us from all unrighteousness.''
If you have some sin that is troubling

you, bring it into the light, and hand it
over to execution; if you do, He is faithful and just. He will pardon you and,
having pardoned it, then He will go to
work and cleanse it—put it out of existence, so it will no longer dominate you;
He will cleanse you from all unrighteousness. So the Word is our laver, and
ever the efficient agent in the hands of
the Holy Ghost.

What is the cleansing here typified?
First, regeneration, giving us a new
nature, a new heart. That comes after
we trust in Jesus, after we come to the
altar of blood, and leave our sins. Then
the blessed Holy Ghost puts into us a
new life and spirit. That is the first
step; it is the washing of regeneration.
But there is a more complete washing
than this; namely, the sanctifying grace
of Jesus Christ. This is the complete
and entire dedication of your whole being to God, by which you become His,
and His alone, and He becomes yours
and fills you with His own nature, and
His own Spirit. He takes possession of
your desires, your will, your affections,

and all the faculties and powers of your being and becomes the dominating, controlling, keeping power of your life, the indwelling Christ, through the Spirit, in your heart. It is not merely that you get a new heart and then go on struggling with a thousand elements of evil, but your whole spirit and soul and body are dedicated to the Lord, preserved blameless unto the coming of the Lord Jesus Christ. Undoubtedly this is set forth in this ancient laver. It was not that the priests got a little cleansing; the laver meant that every spot was taken from their garments, for had there been one blemish there, they could not have dared to enter the Holy Place.

Oh, friends, if this means anything, it means everything! If the Spirit and the blood of Christ can take away one spot, they can take away all; if they can keep you one moment, they can keep you a thousand years; if they can give you a single spark, they can fill you. Suppose the priest had gone up and said, "I will get off one little speck today, and some other day I will cleanse another," what

would have been the consequence if he
had ventured into the Tabernacle? God
says, "Let them wash themselves with
water that they die not." That single
spot of sin would have been a conductor
to receive the flash of the divine anger.
The Spirit of God requires of us and
brings to us, entire cleansing, and the
great hindrance there is to our receiving
it is that we are afraid to believe so great
a Gospel. We are afraid to dare to take
God at His word, and to think that He is
able and willing to do what He says.
"Then will I sprinkle clean water upon
you, and ye shall be clean." I believe,
dear friends, one spot of sin in your
heart will be like one spot of mortifica-
tion in your body. We must get clean.
I do not speak of our mistakes and mis-
apprehensions, but I do speak of standing without any conscious, willful act of
sin. I do not believe that you can go
into the presence of God; I do not believe
that you can have communion with God,
that you can have the peace of God, if
you are tolerating or consenting to anything in your heart or life that you know

to be wrong, and yet saying, ''It is too much to expect God to keep a man like that.'' God says that is the way He is going to keep you, and you and I have no business to belittle His keeping care, and His precious redemption. Let us take Him fully, and while He may see in us ten thousand things we do not see, and while He will lead us ever to a deeper sanctification, this is a very different thing from tolerating evil. I believe God accepts us as pure, when we stand pure in all the light we have, and do all we know of His blessed will.

Beloved, are you fully cleansed this day? Have you come to God's laver to see your whole self, feeling that everything is dependent upon your being right with God? Have you brought everything to Him? Do you with open face and heart take the cleansing water, as well as the cleansing blood, to wash every stain away? Do you believe He does it? And do you hear the Master say, ''Now are ye clean through the word which I have spoken unto you?'' Oh, how touching it is that He said that to poor

Simon Peter, to the very disciples that in twenty-four hours were to sin again! But He cleansed them and they were cleansed, and they believed it; and even if you should slip tomorrow, beloved, take His cleansing today. And if you take Him as Peter might have taken Him, He will keep you from stumbling, and bring you to the presence of His glory at last with exceeding joy.

This leads us to another point; namely, the continual application of the cleansing. Not only was it single cleansing, but it was a very frequent, reiterated ceremony; they had to do it every time they went into the sanctuary, and to the altar. This brings out a very precious truth; that is, the Lord Jesus Christ, after He consecrates us thoroughly and fills us entirely, has still grace to fill us every day, and grace to overcome all the ills and trials of life. I think you will see this better in the eighth verse of the thirteenth chapter of John. There he uses two expressions, for the verbs are different in the original. One describes a thorough cleansing. "He that is washed"

(tenth verse) "needeth not save to wash
his feet."

The word "washed" means he that is
thoroughly washed; that is, entirely
cleansed, soul and body, and thoroughly
sanctified. He does not need to have that
done, but he will need to have his feet
washed, to have the little stains of the
passing earth, the little missteps that
come a thousand times a day, removed.
He does not need to be again saved and
sanctified to God but he needs a thousand
rewashings, from the transient defilements that had not entered his heart but
had stained his feet. He that is washed
needeth not his whole body to be plunged
beneath the stream, but needs to have
the daily defilements removed. You are
washed in this larger sense, but if He
wash you not in this lower sense ye have
no part with Him. Your communion is
interrupted until you are cleansed.

Now, dear friends, this is the meaning
of coming daily to the throne of grace,
and finding help in time of need. This is
the privilege of the most consecrated believer. That blessed laver is open in our

hearts continually and the Great High
Priest is ever there, with the hyssop, to
sprinkle us, and wash us over and over,
even from the very shadow of the faintest
contact that comes from the spirits of
others or the atmosphere of the world
in which we live.

And then what a comfort it is to know
that the water came down to the level of
the priests. I am glad to think they did
not have to climb up to it, but it could
be poured upon their garments by simply
opening the faucets and getting under it.
"Say not in thine heart, Who shall as-
cend into heaven? Or who shall descend
into the deep? But what saith it? The
word is nigh thee, even in thy mouth, and
in thy heart: that is, the word of faith
which we preach; that if thou shalt confess with thy mouth the Lord Jesus, and
shalt believe in thine heart that God hath
raised him from the dead, thou shalt be
saved."

We pass on, just a moment, to glance
at the persons that are to be cleansed.
They were the priests of God, those who
came to minister in the more immediate

presence of God. They were not common
people—the unsanctified crowd; they
were God's consecrated ones, and they
stand for that blessed place of privilege
which all believers may occupy today.
The priesthood of old meant consecrated
service. And so, beloved, this laver, this
sanctifying Christ, this ever cleansing
grace, is given to us that we may use
it in holy service. There was a time, I
suppose, that we felt this sanctifying
grace was given to us to prepare for the
glories of heaven. But I am so glad that
the belief is now going abroad through
the Church that it is not the end but the
beginning of Christian service. The position of this laver was not in the far dis-
tant part, but just beyond the altar of
sacrifice. First, they came to the altar
where they offered their victim, then to
the laver, where they washed away their
stains. It was all before they entered
into the Holy Place, the sanctuary of
God, for His more immediate communion. Now, beloved, this is the meaning
and place of sanctification. Oh, that we
may learn where we stand! Christ does

5

not keep your sanctification until you get to the Holy of Holies. He gives it to you just after you have been pardoned, that you may enter His service, do His consecrated work, and live a life of purity for His glory, and the good of men.

And now, friends, if this be true that God has provided all this for us, what a responsibility it places upon every Christian. Look at it. It is not hidden behind those curtains; it is open to everybody, and so it is open to you. If you do not receive it, what will you say to Christ in the day of His coming, when He asks you, "Friend, wherefore hast thou come in not having thy wedding garment?" What can any Christian say that lives in any sin? I am afraid you would be silent, and have nothing to say. Let us be sure that we have not only come to the altar and the blood, but that we are washed with pure water, and are constantly keeping our garments unspotted from the world, and cleansed in the ever-flowing tides of His love.

We have the altar that tells of His finished work; and we have the fountain that tells of the infinite supply for all our needs. The specific idea of the laver was cleansing. Have we received it? are we walking with the Spirit of God? We have trusted the Saviour; have we likewise trusted the Holy Ghost? We have received the blood. Have we received with equal fullness the boundless supplies of His Spirit? We have prized His love who for thirty-three years dwelt among us as a martyr and an outcast. But have we recognized His equal love, who for eighteen hundred years has made His home with a vile and sinful race, dwelling as one might have dwelt in a leprous hospital, to cleanse away the vileness of our guilt? I am ashamed whenever I think of that love and patience, that I have not loved Him more, and more perfectly yielded to His grace. Oh, this day take the Holy Ghost afresh! Let the vast and mighty floods pour into your nature, and as you go forth, go forth with the blessed consciousness, that through all your soul its waters flow, a stream of heavy cleansing. That laver was ever full. So it stands today; there is enough for all.

And it comes down to the level of every one of us. Mr. Spurgeon tells a quaint and interesting story of his early days. He said when he was a boy, he and his brother had two aunts whom they used to visit. When they went to see Aunt Margaret, they never got many cookies or good things; she had them put away on an upper shelf. But when they went to Aunt Jane's, they got all they wanted; she gave them the right of way, and always put the cookies on the lower shelf.

How near Christ brings salvation! The law puts it away up in Sinai; Moses even could not reach it. But Christ has come to the level of the feeblest child, and put it where anybody can get it, like those ancient waters that flowed down to the foot of the laver so they could reach them. I am so glad that the waters of His love and His cleansing are pouring at your feet. Get under them, dear friend. Take that which God has brought so near and then go into His sanctuary and minister for His glory, and for the sake of a sinful and dying world.

CHAPTER IV.

THE LIGHT.

"And thou shalt make a candlestick of pure gold; of beaten work shall the candlestick be made; his shaft and his branches, his bowls, his knops, and his flowers shall be of the same. And six branches shall come out of the sides of it: three branches of the candlestick out of one side, and three branches of the candlestick out of the other side: three bowls made like unto almonds, with a knop and a flower in one branch; and three bowls made like unto almonds in the other branch, with a knop and a flower: so in the six branches that come out of the candlestick. And in the candlestick shall be four bowls made like unto almonds, with their knops and their flowers. Their knops and their branches shall be of the same; all of it shall be one beaten work of pure gold. And thou shalt make the seven lamps thereof; that they may give light over against it. And the tongs thereof, and the snuffdishes thereof, shall be of pure gold. Of a talent of pure gold shall he make it, with all these vessels. And look that thou make them after their pattern, which was shewed thee in the mount."—Ex. 25: 31. In connection with this read Mat. 5: 16: "Let your light so shine before men, that they may see your good works, and glorify your Father which is in heaven."

THE two figures of light and oil are very beautiful and interesting, even in their natural symbolism. Light was

the first created object of the natural
world, and it is its chief glory. It is
essential, in a great measure, to the existence of life. It is that which clothes
everything with beauty and color. It
is that which gives the glory to the rainbow and the ruby. It is that which makes
the diamond anything but a little bit of
charcoal. It is that which makes the
human face so full of loveliness; and it
is that which gives us everything that
is beautiful in our human relationships,
and in all the wonders of the natural
world. Nor have we only the light which
comes from without, but the light which
comes from within; the sense of sight;
the power of wisdom which brings into
our consciousness and perception the objects of nature around us.

We find this figure through God's
Word from the beginning. It was the
most marked symbol of His presence.
He appeared in the Garden of Eden, in
the light of the Shekinah. He appeared
to Abraham in the lamp that passed between the pieces of the sacrifice. He appeared in the wilderness to the children

of Israel in the pillar of fire. And He
appeared to Moses in the burning bush.
Jesus uses this figure Himself; He
claimed to be the light of the world, and
of His own children especially. The Holy
Spirit is also the source of light. And
the vision of the Apocalypse closes with
the light that is brighter than the sun, and
a rainbow gathering up all its beautiful
effulgence around the throne forever.

And so the figure of oil expresses many
interesting thoughts. It is the source
of artificial light. It contains in itself
the elements of life and healing and, in
contact with fire, the elements of light.
We find it employed for many other purposes than light. It was used in connection with the consecration of the
priesthood, and in healing, but it was
especially set apart for the lighting of
God's sanctuary. And it was specifically
prescribed by God Himself, and by the
most awful sanctions guarded from being
counterfeited. If anyone should endeav-
or to imitate or counterfeit it, he was to
be cut off from among the people. Its
ingredients were compounded together in

some mysterious way for its sacred use, to light God's holy sanctuary.

The two figures of light and oil are combined in the golden candlestick of which we have read a description. It stood within God's ancient sanctuary, the first object which you saw on entering the door on the left. On the other side was the table of shewbread, and just before the altar of incense.

The candlestick was wrought of solid gold worth about forty thousand dollars. A talent of gold was beaten into this piece of exquisite workmanship. It consisted of one stem or branch in the centre with three lateral branches springing from either side, probably a little lower, and it was adorned with three kinds of ornaments, knops, flowers, and bowls like unto almonds. The knops seem to have been fruit, probably pomegranates. Thus each of the branches running upon either side would be adorned with a flower of gold, then a pomegranate a little farther up the branch, and then, on the top, the almond bowl containing the oil with which the light was maintained.

God was very particular in specifying these forms of decoration, and He told Moses to take care to make them after this pattern. All was of the same gold as the central stem. The flowers and knops and lamps were probably very elaborate and beautiful in their construction. Then there was the usual furniture of tongs and snuffers. The lamps were daily replenished with oil by the priests. The candlestick was so valuable that it afterwards became the peculiar temptation of their conquerors, and we find that, when Jerusalem fell, after the time of Christ, this candlestick was one of the spoils of the Roman conquerors. The most vivid recollection that travelers have in remembering the Arch of Titus in Rome, is the carving on that arch of this emblem, carried by several Roman soldiers in the march of triumph. It is said that it was afterwards lost in the Tiber, and has completely disappeared from human knowledge.

It had many important spiritual les-

sons; let us look at some of them. God
does not want His house now to be dec-
orated with costly embellishments; often where these are most lavishly employed His house has been most dishonored. But He wants the pure light
of divine illumination through His word
and Holy Spirit in our hearts and minds,
and this ancient candlestick is the token
of these things. May God teach us something more about it today, and make it
more real to our hearts!

First, it teaches us that Christ is the
light of the world. This figure of light
is constantly appropriated by Him. He
has given the light of reason to the human mind and He it is that brings light
to the new-born soul. In the New Jerusalem He shall be the light thereof. If
you want light in your soul you want
Jesus to come in; He will dispel the darkness, perplexity, and sin, and everything
evil. "God is light, and in him is no
darkness at all."

Again, this tells us that the Holy Ghost
is the instrument of light. While the light
tells us of Christ, the oil tells us of the

Holy Ghost. "The anointing which you have received of him abideth in you." He anointed Jesus of Nazareth with the Holy Ghost. "The Spirit of the Lord is upon me; because the Lord hath anointed me to proclaim good tidings, to preach the gospel to the poor." Jesus was called Christ because He was thus anointed.

And thirdly, the golden candlestick stands not only for Christ and the Spirit, but it also stands for the Church and the Christian. It represents us as the reflectors of His light. It represents us as the sevenfold, complete, light-bearers who give out this reflection to the dark world around us and so become also the lights of the world. "Ye are the light of the world." And, "Let your light so shine before men, that they may see your good works, and glorify your Father which is in heaven."

These, then, are the special points of significance in this ancient type of light: Jesus Christ our perfect light; the Holy Ghost who brings this light and sheds it abroad in our hearts, just as the atmosphere brings yonder light and sheds it abroad through our world; and the believer and the Church of God who hold the light-like candlesticks, bearing it and reflecting it on the darkness of a sinful world.

Now let us gather some of the lessons that come from these lines of truth.

1. The light which God gives to us is all divine, and in no sense human. This oil, as I told you, was not manufactured by any ordinary process nor obtained from any apothecary's dispensary nor any human source; but it was made from materials divinely specified. And so it teaches us that the light we need does not come from man, not from the reasonings of the wise, not from our own soundest judgment even; but it comes to us from Jesus Christ and His precious Word. And all the light that God gives a soul in its heavenly journey must be divine.

2. Again, there was no light in the ancient Tabernacle but from this. There were no windows; the candlestick was the sole illumination of God's sanctuary.

And so it teaches us that we have no other light but God. When we trust Him, we must wholly trust Him. "Trust in the Lord with all thine heart, and lean not to thine own understanding." Have you this light? Have you taken all your ideas of things from the Bible, and from the Spirit, and from God? Is your Tabernacle partly lighted by the golden lights, and partly by the murky light of the world? I do not wonder that it gets dark sometimes. Let us look and see if we have the light after the pattern on the mount. A great many Christians go astray here. They are not careful to have all their light from above.

3. Again, we learn from the ancient candlestick that the light which God gives us is a perfect light. It was a sevenfold light, and seven, you know, stands for completeness. There was not one only, but there were seven, and they afforded all the light that was required. And so God gives you light that has no darkness in it. When He leads you, you will find at last that it is always in the right path. And when He teaches, you can lean

your whole weight on Him, for He cannot fail. "God is light, and in him there is no darkness at all."

So the Holy Ghost is called "the seven Spirits before the throne." There is the spirit of peace, the spirit of sonship, the spirit of joy, the spirit of love, the spirit of trust, the spirit of prayer, the spirit of holiness, the spirit of power; these are all different forms of light, but they are all the same divine light. So God has a great many kinds of light. He has the light by day, and the light by night. He is the light that guides, and the light that glorifies. He is the light that shines in with awful power upon your sins and makes you weep. And then He is the light that shines upon His own sweet face, His own precious Cross and blood, and lifts you out of your sin, and makes your heart happy in His joy. Sometimes the light shines from His truth, and then sometimes from the Spirit's presence in the inner life—

> "Sometimes this light surprises
>   The Christian while He sings,
> It is the Lord who rises
>   With healing in His wings."

And sometimes we cannot keep it in,
but it shines out and sheds its glory on
others—the sevenfold light of God in the
heart.

4. Again, this light revealed the other
objects in the Tabernacle. It showed
these priests the beautiful and precious
things all around. It revealed to them
the table, covered with the bread and
the frankincense. The best thing in the
light was that it showed, not the light,
but the bread. And so when this light
comes, it is not that you have such a light
that you gaze until your eyes are dazzled;
but the light comes to show you the bread
of life; to show how the promises
are for you; how you are to understand;
how you are to take; how you are to
hold fast and be strong. And the whole
plan of divine redemption becomes personal to you. The grace of Jesus Christ
fills your whole being and you wonder
why you could not have taken Him more
fully before, it seems so easy now to feed
on Christ and appropriate His promises.
Why, you have got the light; it is shin-

ing on the table, and all is easy and plain.

And then you can perceive and receive the frankincense as well as the bread, and absorb all its sweetness into your finer sensibilities. You know what this means, dear friends. Here is not only bread, but something else you need. I used to want the light, to have a glorious experience. But I am so glad now to get the light to show me how to live on Christ, the light that I do not look much at for its own glory, but which I look at for its value. If we looked at the light all the time in its full glare, it would be painful; but He gives us in nature the wholesome light with its sober shades as well as its sunlit glories, which shows us our daily footseps, and is to us the light of life. I think it is a dangerous thing to be always wanting pyrotechnic displays. It is far better to get the light of the sober day, which shows you how to live.

5. Again, the candlestick showed itself. "The candlestick shall give light over against itself." It was to show

its own branches, as well as the other objects. It was to show that it was all right, that it was pure gold, that it was burning steadily. It was to show the beautiful flowers, the pomegranate fruit, the almond bowls at the top, filled with oil for lighting, the Tabernacle. ''Over against itself.'' And so, dear child of God, you want to have light to show that you are living right, to show the blossoms of your faith and hope, to show the pomegranate fruits that make your Christian life a blessing to others, and to show the almond bowls that hold the oil, not only to light your own path but the path of those around you. Does this light show you to be like Himself, beaten out of the same piece of gold and adorned with all the beauties and graces of the Holy Spirit?

6. Again, this light required to be daily replenished, both by filling the lamps with oil, and by using the snuffers to snuff off the excrescences. Every day the the priest poured in the oil, took away the exhausted wick, and kept it clean and pure. And so God has to use His

6

snuffers, and fill us with the Holy Spirit. You and I can only shine with love when we are filled with love. We must keep daily supplied with His light, and we must see that the little hindrances are cut off. Have you a pair of snuffers? Have you taken away all the burned-out dross from your lamp? Have you the heavenly oil? If you are not shining, something is in the way.

7. And again, the candlestick did not have inherent light; it was only the bearer of the light; it only held the light, but the oil gave the light. And so you and I are not the light; Jesus Christ is our light, and we simply receive and reflect Him.

This is the secret of all holiness. I am not light myself and I am not expected to have light in my person; but I just have Him, and show Him forth. He is the light that shines from my eyes, my manner, my tone, and I am the mere candlestick to let others see Him. I do not stand before the world and tell them that I am strong but I tell them that Christ is strong, and that I use His

strength. I do not tell them that I am
wise but that Christ is wise, and I just
use His wisdom. I have not faith but
Christ has faith, and I draw from it
moment by moment to glorify Him and
not myself. I am not love, and never
expect to love by my own impulses as
God expects me to. But Jesus is the
heart of love; Jesus is love itself, and
Jesus is mine; His love is mine; I draw
it in and give it out, and hold His love
before the world, and say, "He enables
me to love as He loves, and yet without
Him I should be a loveless lump of clay.
I think that is what the Master meant
when He said, "Let your light so shine
before men, that they may see your good
works, and glorify your Father which is
in heaven." You are to glorify God, not
yourself. They will not say, "What a
wonderful man that is; what a remarkable Christian that is; what a pure spirit; what a gifted mind!" Oh, no! but they
will say: "How full he is of Christ;
why cannot I be as he? He tells me
he is as weak as I am, but God supplies
his daily needs. Now, why cannot I do

the same?" Now, this is what I mean by holding up the light of Jesus and letting it so shine before men that they will say, "This is the grace of God and I may have it, too."

8. Zechariah gives us a description of this candlestick in which there are several points that we do not find in any other, and one of the most beautiful is that these candlesticks were not replenished by mechanical means, but the different bowls were supplied with oil by two olive trees that grew on either side and seemed to distil the very substance of their fruit, and to press out the oil just as fast as it was needed, without effort, into the lamps, and to keep them filled. This is an exquisite picture, the lamp not needing to be filled, but filling itself, as the pipes were always open. Beloved, that is the way we can be linked with Him, so that, breath by breath, we shall be filled with Him.

There is one olive tree on one side, the Lord Jesus Christ, and on the other side the Holy Spirit, both pouring their life into our souls and bodies and impart-

ing themselves to us every moment. It
it not a blessing that we get once in a
while, but a constant connection and com-
munication.

So let us draw near to him; so let
us go forth to abide in Him; so let us
have His light and His life, and then
we cannot help shining, because we shall
by just like Himself. And in His over-
flowing life we shall be a blessing to
others even greater than the blessing we
receive. Oh, may He come to us now
and light up the sanctuary of our heart
until it shall shine like the chambers
above! May He reveal to us the heavenly bread until we shall eat and be satisfied! May He open to our vision the
golden altar of intercession and incense
and even the rent veil just beyond, His
own immediate, everlasting presence
chamber, for His own dear name's sake!
Amen!

CHAPTER V.

THE SHEWBREAD.

"Thou shalt also make a table of shittim wood: two cubits shall be the length thereof, and a cubit the breadth thereof, and a cubit and a half the height thereof. And thou shalt overlay it with pure gold, and make thereto a crown of gold round about. And thou shalt make unto it a border of a hand-breadth round about, and thou shalt make a golden crown to the border thereof round about. And thou shalt make for it four rings of gold, and put the rings in the four corners that are on the four feet thereof. Over against the border shall the rings be for places of the staves to bear the table. And thou shalt make the staves of shittim wood, and overlay them with gold, that the table may be borne with them. And thou shalt make the dishes thereof, and spoons thereof, and covers thereof, and bowls thereof, to cover withal; of pure gold shalt thou make them. And thou shalt set upon the table shewbread before me always.

"And thou shalt take fine flour, and bake twelve cakes thereof: two tenth deals shall be in one cake. And thou shalt set them in two rows, six on a row, upon the pure table before the Lord. And thou shalt put pure frankincense upon each row, that it be on the bread for a memorial, even an offering made by fire unto the Lord. Every sabbath he shall set it in order before the Lord continually, being taken from the children of Israel by an everlasting covenant. And it shall be Aaron's and his sons'; and they shall eat it in the holy place; for it is

86

most holy unto him of the offerings of the Lord made
by fire by a perpetual statute.

"For my flesh is meat indeed, and my blood is
drink indeed. He that eateth my flesh, and drinketh
my blood, dwelleth in me, and I in him. As the
living Father hath sent me, and I live by the Father;
so he that eateth me, even he shall live by me. This is
that bread which came down from heaven: not as
your fathers did eat manna, and are dead: he that
eateth of this bread shall live forever."—Ex. 25: 23-
30; Lev. 24: 5, 9; John 6: 55-58.

RIGHT across the Tabernacle, on our
right as we enter, and in the full
blaze of the golden candlestick, which
almost seems to shine for the purpose
of revealing it alone, stands the table of
shewbread, which these verses describe
and whose significance they explain.

It is a simple little table three feet
long by half that width, and two feet
three inches high, made of acacia wood
and overlaid with gold.

Upon it there ever stand twelve loaves
of unleavened bread, covered with fine
powdered frankincense, offered before
the Lord continually, as a memorial.
Every Sabbath these loaves are renewed,
the old ones being eaten by the priests
in the Holy Place, while the frankincense

is burned before the Lord on the golden altar of incense.

Beside the loaves are trays and vessels of wine, also offered before the Lord as a drink-offering and drunk by the priests on the Sabbath in the sanctuary.

This familiar type is so natural and expressive that there can be no doubt of its significance, and no difficulty in apprehending its beauty and fitness. As water and light are the natural symbols of cleansing and illumination, so bread as fittingly expresses the satisfaction and provision for the soul's deeper need which Christ supplies and the Gospel reveals. The same symbolical idea was presented previously in the manna, which fell for forty years in the wilderness, and which, we are distinctly told, was designed to show them "that man shall not live by bread alone, but by every word of God." In the bread and wine of the Lord's Supper, the same element is preserved as the perpetual symbol to the Church of Christ's provision for His people's need.

Our Saviour has claimed this symbol

for Himself in the sixth chapter of John,
and shown how fittingly it expresses the
real life which the soul can find only in
His life and death, and His living life-
giving Person, of which, indeed, it would
seem to be not too much to say that all
natural elements were made to be the
symbols and foreshadowings. This is but
the figure, He is the real Bread. His flesh
is meat indeed, and His blood is drink
indeed.

I. *The Preparation of the Bread.*—
There is much in this symbol which nat-
urally suggests the deepest and holiest
mysteries of Christ's person and work.

Bread is the fruit of the ground, which
was cursed for man's sin. So Christ
was born of a cursed and sinful race,
and came under that curse to become
the life and support of the human soul.
Bread is the offspring of death. The
seed must be buried in the soil and die
ere it can produce the harvest which
feeds the face.

So Christ Himself has appropriated
this beautiful figure, and taught us that,
as the corn of wheat by dying grows

into ampler life, so He was planted in death in the soil of Calvary, that from that dark sepulchre He might come forth in resurrection life as the life of the world.

Is it pressing the symbol too far to say that as bread must be crushed in the mill stones and kneaded in the baker's hand and baked in the fierce heat of the oven, so our heavenly bread has been perfected and prepared under the crushing pressure and in the consuming flame of suffering?

And as in the natural world life is maintained not by direct impartation of power, but in the concrete form of bread, so the soul's life is not received direct from God, but in the Person of Christ.

The loaves must be prepared; so the Bread of life must be presented in a form in which we can partake of it, not wheat, not flour, not dough, but bread. So divine truth and grace must be adapted to human need. All truth is not bread. Much preaching and teaching is but presenting ears of corn, husks, barbs, beards, and all often. A divine relation of God would not have been bread for a dying one; it needed a concrete redemption and revelation, a person who would gather up and concentrate in himself all that God is to a lost humanity, truth incarnate, the Gospel of a personal, loving, suffering, sin-atoning Saviour.

There were twelve loaves, ample provision for all the tribes. So Christ is our all-sufficient Saviour. Special provision is made for each tribe. Not one loaf for all, but personal provision for each one. That is the way Christ saves. Not all men in the mass, but each one separately, ''He tasted death for every man.'' He has a loaf for everyone of you. There is for you in the heart of God, in the work of Christ, in the thoughts of your Lord, in the prepared places of heaven, a place as specific as if you were the only one for whom He died and lives. Oh, how touching this individual love of my Redeemer for me! How encouraging to me to claim my share, for it is all for me! I am depriving none by receiving all, I am enriching none by declining anything.

The bread was unleavened. Not loaves, but cakes, because the process of fermentation was the symbol of sin and decay. The priests of God must eat incorruptible bread. The reason why so many are weak and sickly is that they used the leavened bread of human pleasure, pride, sin. ''Labor not for the meat which perisheth, but for that which endureth.''

II. *The Offering of the Bread.*—Before the bread was eaten by man, it was first offered to God for seven days as a meat-offering.

So Christ's work of salvation was as much as an offering to God as a provision for man. We lose sight of this. There were necessities on the divine side as well as the human. There was a law dishonored; there was a love unyielded; there was a holiness offended with impurity and sin. There was a Father's heart deserving the love and obedience of a race He had created in His image. And Christ came to answer

all these divine requirements even more
than to meet human misery with full
blessings. Christ came as man's answer
to God as much as God's message to
man. Christ came by His blood to meet
the holy demands of justice, by His
obedience to meet the claims of law, by
His consecrated love to meet the long-
ing of God's heart for love, by His purity and righteousness to satisfy the holiness of God and to do all this, as a man.
So that in Him God saw man cancelling
his own sin, bearing its righteous penalty, receiving and obeying His law, loving
and submitting to His will, yielding himself a living offering of love on the altar
of sacrifice, and presenting a character
so pure and holy that it was the reflection of His own, and in it He was satisfied. He looked past the men that had
sinned and were sinning and saw only
the one man that stood for them, and in
Him He accepts all. It was an infinite
satisfaction to His blessed nature and
character. It was the bread of God as
well as that of man. It was a sacrifice
to God of a sweet-smelling savor, and

His infinite being went out crying: "My
beloved Son, in whom I am well pleased."
And all of us who are in Him are thus
accepted through Him; His person, character, and work, are substitute for ours,
and we are accepted in the Beloved.

And so far as His life and spirit live
in us, we, too, like Him, are an offering
to God, acceptable to Him. As man lives
on God and finds in Him his life, so God
lives in His children and has in them
His life, His bread. So in Rev. 3: 20
the feast is described: "I will sup with
him, and he with me."

Hence, we find our Saviour always
representing His work as done prima-
rily, for His Father, His will, His glory,
His pleasure; and so also, before He
meets with His disciples or allows their
communion He must rise to His Father's
presence and present His finished work.
"Touch me not," He says to Mary, "for
I am not yet ascended to my Father."
The bread must first be offered on the
heavenly table ere it can be partaken
of by the earthly children. The Head of
the table, the Father, must first partake

of the feast of salvation ere His children
can receive the cup of salvation. But
this once done, we find Him afterwards,
not only permitting but commanding
their touch, giving Himself to the touch
of doubting Thomas, and bidding Peter
and the other ten on the Galilean shore
to that morning meal which was the type
of the table now open to His loving children, and the bread accepted in heaven
and offered on earth to all who hunger.

III. *The Eating of the Bread.*—On the
Sabbath day the old loaves were removed
and eaten by the priest, and new ones
placed on the table. So while Christ is,
in the first aspect of His work, an offering to God, He is, in the second, a
provision for His people's need.

The spiritual meaning of this language
none but a Christian can understand.
And to a true believer, to a soul that has
felt the deep inner need of Christ and
known its satisfaction, to a soul that
is living in communion with the Person
of Jesus Christ, to a soul that has felt
the crushing sense of sin and then the
sweetness of assured pardon and peace

by His Spirit's voice, to a soul which
has felt the utter disappointment of human enjoyment, and the bitter pain of
human sorrow, and then after all this
found the real, deep, satisfying sweetness of his consolations, to a soul that
has found these promises, commands,
directions, more precious than gold, and
more necessary than food, and this Gospel more interesting than romance, and
back of all this Gospel and these words,
has felt its way to the living Person of
Jesus, and knows what it is or anything
of what it is to have Him as an all-sufficient Saviour, a perpetual Presence, a
very pleasant help, and a friend more
near and loved than human affection can
comprehend, to a soul that has known
any or all of this as hundreds of sym-
pathetic hearts today do know, it would
be idle to attempt to interpret and il-
lustrate such words as these: "I am the
Bread of life, he that cometh to me shall
never hunger, and he that believeth in
me shall never thirst. I am the Living
Bread. He that eateth my flesh dwelleth
in me and I in him.   My flesh is meat

indeed, and my blood is drink indeed.''
The golden key that unlocks their mystery is in the secret place of your own heart.

This bread was eaten by the priests alone. They were the types of all true believers, so all Christians, all true believers, and they only, can feed upon Christ. None others understand it. None others desire it. None others have either appetite or organs to appropriate Him. It was a beautiful provision, that while the blemished and feeble were not permitted to minister at God's altar of incense, they were not to be hindered from eating the bread in the Holy Place. So although you may be too weak a Christian to do any useful ministry for Christ, although you may be to inconstant and unbelieving and cold even to offer acceptable worship, you are not thereby cut off from the provisions of God's house. Christ wants especially to feed and cherish the faint one. Come and feed on Him till you get strong, and hands and feet and voice and tongue can join without blemish in His service, too.

7

The bread was eaten on the Sabbath, perhaps a type of the special provision God makes for His children on His own day. Here is the family table and the day of peculiar Christian nourishing. He who can afford to lose it, will find himself ill prepared for the conflicts and tasks of life. But it is almost as fatal an error to make this the only day of spiritual renewing, as to neglect it altogether.

Every day requires new strength, and grace, and one must have "daily bread." The whole of the true believer's life is a Sabbath in the sense that he has entered into rest, rest from sin and self in Christ, and in the enjoyment of His peace he can sing: "I shall not want. He maketh me to lie down in green pastures. He leadeth me by the waters of rest." Have you learned to know this Sabbath, and found in Christ this Living Bread?

IV. *The Wine.*—Life needs more than bare support. It requires cordials for the faint, refreshment for the feeble, and the festival for the glad and the gay. The Gospel has provision for the higher

capacities and more special needs of man.
Talk of the wine of life that flows in
the rich, full tides of tumultuous human
passion, and the veins of youth and love
of genius. There are deep and holy joys;
there are everlasting consolations; there
are raptures of love and hope and communion; there are hours of peace sur-
passing all understanding; there are il-
luminations of soul, and visions of truth,
and unfoldings of God, and foredawn-
ings of heaven, and there are tides of
power and glory that touch and thrill
all that is divine in the soul, until all
other life seems a living death, and death
is life in the glory revealed. Oh! there
is wine, wine on the lees well refined,
as well as bread in the house of God, and
he who has drunk of it once will say to
the Master of the Feast: "Thou hast
kept the good wine until now."

V. *The Frankincense.*—This was the
symbol of acceptance. It was burned on
the altar while the priests partook of the
bread, and sent up its sweet perfume
through all the Holy Place.

The first truth this suggested was the

sweet acceptance by God of Christ's
work. It is not only offered, but accepted.

The second truth was the acceptance of
the sacred meal of the priests as an act
of worship. God accepted them in eating
it. There is no more acceptable service
you can render to God that to feed upon
Christ and rejoice in Him. Martha covered her groaning table with viands for
her God, but Mary pleased Him more as
she sat at His feet and heard His words,
feeding on His life and love, and wor-
shiping Him by receiving what He gave.

VI. *The Table.*—Its purpose was to ex-
hibit the bread. This is what the Church
and ministry are appointed to do. This
is what we are trying to do today. What
lessons we may learn from this table!

It was simple. It had but one use, not
to show itself, but the bread. So the
ministry is out of place when its brilliancy obscures the Saviour. When the
great Italian painter had finished his
picture of the Last Supper, he showed
it to a friend. "What beautiful cups"
was the answer. The painter drew his

brush over the canvas with a shadow
of sorrow on his brow. He had failed.
He had painted the cups, but not the
Saviour. Many a sermon is but an exhibition of pictorial skill in painting
cups, and the Saviour is in the back-
ground. May God make us like the table,
only exhibiting the bread!

It was for the purpose of holding forth
the bread as an offering to God as well
as for the priest's use, so the highest
aim in all our ministry should be to
hold Christ forth for God's glory as much
as man's good. If you speak Christ, if
you live Christ so that God sees Him in
you, it is heaven enough, if no man re-
joices. If I have held Christ up so that
God is satisfied, even if you do not eat
the bread, my ministry is not amiss.

Our first aim should be for God. The
table, however, was meant also to hold
the bread which the priests were to partake of. And so we must offer Christ to
the world. But let us learn the lesson of
the loaves and the frankincense. *Loaves,*
not ears of corn, nor lumps of dough,
nor bushels of grain—but bread, pre-

pared for the soul's present need—compact, concrete, warm, simple, and in small quantities.

And frankincense, attractive, sweet, appetizing, so that they will eat and live. Not the loaves without the frankincense.

In conclusion, what is all this to you? Are you living on the bread of God or starving, while, in the Father's house, there is bread and to spare? The blight of the Church today is spiritual exercise and starvation. Men are feeding, or rather famishing, on German Rationalism, French Socialism, and American Sensationalism, on lifeless protoplasms, and juiceless bonds and bank notes, and unwholesome pleasures. "Wherefore do ye spend money for that which is not bread, and your labor for that which satisfieth not! Eat ye that which is good, and let your soul delight itself in fatness."

Is there a hungry soul reading this? Christ stands at the door and knocks. He wants to enter to spread a feast, to sup with you, for your salvation will be meat and drink to Him, and then to have

you sup with Him on the rich blessings
of grace now, and at the banquet of glory
forevermore.

CHAPTER VI.

The Incense.

"And thou shalt make an altar to burn incense upon; of shittim wood shalt thou make it. A cubit shalt be the length thereof, and a cubit the breadth thereof; foursquare shall it be: and two cubits shall be the height thereof: the horns thereof shall be of the same. And thou shall overlay it with pure gold, the top thereof, and the sides thereof round about, and the horns thereof: and thou shalt make unto it a crown of gold round about. And two golden rings shalt thou make to it under the crown of it, by the two corners thereof, upon the two sides of it shalt thou make it; and they shall be for places for the staves to bear it withal. And thou shalt make the staves of shittim wood, and overlay them with gold. And thou shalt put it before the vail that is by the ark of testimony, before the mercy seat that is over the testimony, where I will meet with thee. And Aaron shall burn thereon sweet incense every morning: when he dresseth the lamps, he shall burn incense upon it. And when Aaron lighteth the lamps at even, he shall burn incense upon it; a perpetual incense before the Lord throughout your generation. Ye shall offer no strange incense thereon, nor burnt sacrifice, nor meat offering; neither shall ye pour drink offering thereon. And Aaron shall make an atonement upon the horns of it once in a year with the blood of the sin offering of atonements: once in a year shall he make atonement upon it, throughout your generations: it is most holy unto the Lord."

"And the Lord said unto Moses, Take unto thee sweet spices, stacte, and onycha, and galbanum; these

104

sweet spices, with pure frankincense: of each shall
there be a like weight: and thou shalt make it a
perfume, a confection after the art of the apothecary, tempered together, pure and holy. And thou
shalt beat some of it very small, and put it before
the testimony in the tabernacle of the congregation,
where I will meet with thee: it shall be unto you
most holy. And as for the perfume which thou shalt
make, ye shall not make to yourselves according to
the composition thereof: it shall be unto thee holy
for the Lord. Whosoever shall make like unto that,
to smell thereto, shall even be cut off from his people.''—Ex. 30: 1-11 and 34-end.

THIS is an account of the altar of
incense, the golden altar. It was the
third article of furniture in the sanctuary, and stood at the farther end of
the Holy Place, as one entered the inner
shrine, the Holy of Holies. There, over
against the costly curtains, stood this
altar, and when the incense was burning
upon it, it filled both chambers and made
them fragrant with perfume. It was very
simple in its construction, three feet in
height, and eighteen inches in breadth,
made of costly acacia wood, and covered
with a crown of gold around to keep the
incense from falling off. The incense itself was most costly and precious, pos-
sessing special sacredness, and preserved

by divine sanctions from being counterfeited, or from ordinary use.

What was the special symbolism of
this little altar in the ancient worship?

First, it represented Christ's intercession for us, and also our intercession
in the name of Christ. It is expressive
of prayer and communion with God.
There is something in the sense of smell,
which is perhaps finer than any other of
the senses. The perfume which this sense
appropriates is almost like the breath of
Nature, expressing, it would almost seem,
the finer sensibilities of the soul of the
natural world. And so fragrance has
become the expression of the very out-
breathing of prayer and love. The sweet
breath of burning spices speaks of the
sweet breath of prayer, and is the chosen
emblem of the heart's homage to our
heavenly Father.

But as the very highest example of
prayer is the Son of man, so first it
stands for the prayers of Jesus Christ.
All through His life we see Him praying,
and as His life is closing, it becomes the
culmination of His ministry. As He

crosses the brook Kedron, He is in
prayer. In the garden He prays; on the
Cross He prays; and as He passes from
earth, we know He is exalted at God's
right hand, there to engage in the un-
ceasing work of intercession, for He
"ever liveth to make intercession for
us."

So, on this ancient altar, the ascending
incense continually filling the sacred
chamber, was the type of Christ. His
whole being was one breath of love,
sweetness, and consecration to God, and
remembrance of us, His dear children.
And, expressive thus of His intercession,
it fittingly becomes the example for our
imitation and the pattern of our prayer,
of our communion with God, of that sacred place where "spirits blend, and
friend holds fellowship with friend," and
where every heavenly blessing can be
brought down by the prayer of faith.
Let us think in connection with this altar
of these two things,—of Christ who at
God's right hand is remembering you
and me, and on His uplifted hands presenting our names for acceptance with

God and, also, of our spirit's communion with God. Sweeter than the air of
that ancient Tabernacle may your whole
spirit be baptized, your inmost being
perfumed with devotion until God will
come down to dwell in the delightful
place; and they shall gather, as we read
in the book of Revelation, in phials, the
prayers of the saints, as sweet odors
with which He refreshes even His own
heart, amid the glories of the celestial
courts.

Now, then, all the lessons connected
with this ancient altar may be applied
to these two thoughts—Christ's intercession for us, and our prayers and intercessions in His name.

1. The altar was of incorruptible wood
and incorruptible gold.

Our blessed Lord has a twofold nature. He is divine, and yet He has a
perfect humanity. The wood represents
His humanity, the gold His Divinity. So
the believer has a human and a divine
nature; human, and yet a partaker of the
divine nature. If you have received the
cleansing and sanctifying nature of the

Lord Jesus Christ, you may claim participation in this double life. It is, indeed a great mystery. It would be an awful blasphemy, if not founded on His Word. But every Christian is born of God. His new nature, like that acacia wood, is incorruptible, and like that more precious gold, he possesses the very life and spirit of the Deity Himself.

2. Again, the altar was the highest object in the Tabernacle, several inches higher than the table of shewbread, the laver, or the brazen altar of sacrifice, showing us that prayer is the most exalted ministry in the universe, and that you get higher when you get down on your knees, than at any other times in your existence.

3. Again, this altar was crowned. We observed how the table was crowned. So was this altar. It means that Christ as our High Priest, is a crowned Priest. He is not pleading with uncertainty, but with victory. He is not saying, "I wish it might be"; but, "Father, I will that those which thou has given me be with me. Father, I will that Peter's

faith fail not. Father, I will that this
child shall overcome today.'' And he
shall; it is a royal priesthood, and it is
for you today beloved. So, dear ones,
you, too, have a royal priesthood. You can
come into the presence of God, crowned.
You can feel you are so near the King
that you can ask special favors, and thus
your prayer be a constant ministry for
others. Oh, that you might realize this
and, like Esther before Ahasuerus, know
that you have the power to claim blessing for those who have not the power!
Lord, help us to be true to this ministry,
this authoritative asking, this crowned
priesthood of which the Master says,
"When ye pray, believe that ye receive
the things that you ask, and ye shall have
them." "Thus saith the Lord, concerning my servants, command ye me."
"Whosoever shall say unto this moun-
tain: be thou removed, and be thou cast
into the sea; and shall not doubt in his
heart, but shall believe that those things
which he saith shall come to pass, he
shall have whatsoever he saith." It is
the royal sceptre of intercession, and

Jesus says to us: "I have ordained that ye shall go forth and bring forth fruit, and that whatsoever ye shall ask the Father in my name He may give it to you." He expects you to triumph in this ministry, to take up the crown of prayer which He wears, and shares with you.

4. Again, the next thing about this altar was the horns. It had four, one on each corner, pointing to the four points of the compass, and to the different camps of Israel. There were four great camps; and so the prayer of our Lord reaches north, and south, and east, and west. It is for all His people, and for all the ages of His Church, and for all the quarters of the globe where they may be; for nowhere can we be isolated from His sympathy and His victorious help. It reaches us this moment; it is pointing this very moment to your need, and saying, "Father, deliver! Father, give the victory! Oh, think of that horned altar, the symbol of victory over your enemies, and claim triumph for us!" Rise up, and praise and trust Him for it.

So should it be with our prayers: we must be very wide in the circle of our prayers. Keep out of the ruts of self-ishness. We must enlarge our souls. A brother said the other afternoon: "I have found the outlet—to pray for others." When your heart is pent up and likely to burst, this is the outlet— pray for somebody else. Let your sympathy be very wide; let it have its objects in every land and on every continent. You can have souls in Africa, as well as here, and if every moment of your life is spent in prayer, you shall find when you get home that you have multitudes of souls. Prayer is the greatest of our ministries. It is much more than preaching. Your position in the pews is not less important than mine. I am sure that even in our work, that is the best thing we can do for God. I remember a service in the West from which I saw no fruits. I had prayed so much for this particular work and yet it seemed vain. In rather a tired moment yesterday, I took up some letters, and I found wonderful testimony from that meeting, of one and another that had been saved there and had gone from that place stricken with a sense of guilt, and spoken to others, and they, too, had been saved. Then I felt, in the work of the Gospel there is no power but God; we must trust Him, and expect the things we ask. The great question is—what is God going to do? It is very little matter how you are going to be impressed by what man may say, whether it seems very bright or very dull; but how is the Holy Ghost going to make you feel your need, and arouse you to victory? It is the Holy Ghost claimed by prayer that is the secret of success.

5. Again, there were rings on this golden altar by which it was carried from place to place. I am so glad of that. It was not stationary at one point so that people had to make pilgrimages to it, but it went with the camp. So it is with us. There is not a place on the journey where our altar does not come and turn Jacob's stony pillar into a ladder up to heaven. Do you carry your altar with you, beloved? Have you rings in your

8

altar of prayer? Do you take it with you to business? Do you take it with you on your visits and holidays and picnics? God expects you to be just as near Him on your half-holiday as you are to-day. Have you the rings? And have you the staves in the rings? Can you pray anywhere? Have you learned to let the curtains down and get alone with God at any time?

6. Again, the fire on the altar was always burning, and the sweet spices, too, and the incense was continually rising. And so the Lord Jesus is all the time praying for you. You slept all the night, but all the time He was praying. You awoke, but He was there. It is one of of the sweetest experiences of my life to awake and feel Him so near. It is delightful sometimes to have something brought to your mind by Him, that you would have forgotten and realize that He is ever remembering you.

And how often our hearts get oppressed with the burden that presses us to pray! It is Jesus praying for us. The fire is burning, the incense ascending.

You may not say words all the time, but the incense can rise. Evaporation is going up to the heavens all the time in nature, even when you do not see it go. You see the mist in the morning, and not at noon, but there is twice as much then, because there is more heat, yet you don't see it. So you can all the time be breathing up to God the homage of your heart.

You say—how can I put my whole heart in my business, and pray? You can. I used to be very fond of gardening. I could work in the garden and yet smell the roses; they did not keep me from my husbandry; I had my sweet flowers every second; they did not hinder the work a bit. So you can be busy all the time and have the breath of heaven; it will not hinder you. It is like working in a perfumed room, every sense exhilarated. It is something deeper than prayer—communion. It is like the mother and child, or friends sitting together as I have seen them for hours, and not a word said, but they feel each other's presence. So Christ is with you; you do not talk but there is communion. This is the right state of heart to live in. Oh, it will make the tenement house a sweet place to you! It will put zest in the hospital work for you, dear sister; and even in the nastier work, as you go to the wash tub, my dear woman, it will make the kitchen a palace chamber. And as we meet with the presence even of sin, it will be like a heavenly disinfectant; we can work in any atmosphere. We feel as we go down to our mission work as if we should choke from the evil atmosphere around us, the filthiness of men's hearts and the grossness of sin. But if we have the golden altar with us, and the sweet incense of prayer, we shall be lifted above it and the desert shall blossom as the rose.

7. Again, we read that there was no incense without the fire. And so Christ's intercession for us had to be preceded by the fire of suffering. It is not the prayer that saves us, but the death. It is because He died to make the atonement that now He claims the blessings to be delivered. So we read here that

Aaron was to make an atonement upon
the horns of the altar once a year. Prayer
is not enough. There must be fire. Dear
friends, all the seclusion of the Buddhist,
or the prayers and scourgings of the as-
cetic will not save without the fire. So
the fire of suffering was the first preparation for the intercession work of the
ancient priest.

Then this fire also represents the Holy
Spirit; the Holy Ghost is represented
to us as the Spirit of prayer. It is the
Holy Ghost that brings down to our
hearts the desires that God would make
us feel and prompts in our souls the
inclination, and the sense of need. Oh,
how easy it is to pray when we are just
carried on His wings, when our souls
float out on the breath of God and we
feel that God must give, because God
Himself has already asked! It is He
that breathed it up to heaven, and He
will pour it back. Blessed Spirit of
prayer! Do not discourage Him; listen,
and He will come and come until He
will do all your praying, and it will be
divine. Blessed prayer! it will not be

the cold form of nice words, but the burning incense of a heart that cannot keep it back.

8. Again, I come to the most beautiful of all these symbols; that is the incense itself. It consisted of four parts. Three we do not know. One we do. The frankincense is the gum of an Arabian tree and an object of commerce. The other three we do not know. And so we are taught that in the intercession of our Lord, there are some things we do not know. There is His human nature which we understand, which may stand for the frankincense; but there are the divine things like the unknown spices; we cannot measure their depth nor height. And then, it may teach us that in our prayers there are things we know and things we don't know. There ought always to be definiteness in our prayers; often we may know what is according to His will and expect it. But perhaps the largest part of our praying in the Holy Ghost will be like the three unknown spices; we cannot tell just what the cry means, but we shall be conscious of a cry that

cannot be articulated; we shall feel—
God knows it; it is articulated in His
ear and He will give us the answer, and
show us in due time. This will, perhaps,
help you to understand many of your per-
plexing burdens of prayer. Sometimes
God lets you know, but many times you
cannot. There has been that unutterable
outreaching which seemed incapable of
interpretation or understanding, a
prayer that you did not comprehend and
did not need to know. Sometimes you
feel God is averting some danger, or
saving some dear one, or blessing some
special work, or carrying something
through a crisis. There are days that
will come that you feel if you let go,
something will give way and be lost to
the cause of Christ forever more. In
yonder battlefield the officers and the
privates do not understand the plan of
the battle, but the commanding officer
does and, when the battle is over, they,
too, shall understand it. So let us trust
it all to our Captain and, although we
do not know it all now, we shall here-
after. And God will bring us many an

enraptured soul and say, "That was the soul born of your prayer"; or show us many a glorious issue of His work and say, "That was the work you held up to me."

9. But there is this most beautiful thing I want you not to miss. He says, "Take some of this perfume and beat it very small, and put it before the testimony in the Tabernacle of the congregation, where I will meet with thee." Some of these grains of frankincense, and galbanum were to be pulverized, then they were to be burned in the little grate and go up so sweetly, not one grain lost. O, beloved, there is no little petition, there is no little heartache, there is no little desire too small for Jesus to pray about or you to pray about! That finely powdered incense just means the needs of your life all broken up, and yet each one gathered by Jesus Christ in its minutiæ and presented to the Father with the same care as though it were the fortunes of a kingdom. It cannot be trifling; nothing that is passing through your thoughts is too small for Christ to

pray about, or for you to go to God about. That is the way to make God familiar, and to make common things real —by burning them on God's altar. God help us to bring the little things of life to His mercy-seat.

10. Finally, the position of this altar was significant. It was between the two chambers. It was in the earthly, but it touched the vail, and its incense went into the heavenly. Those two chambers represented earth and heaven. The outer chamber was the believer's life in its earthly experience, and the inner chamber was the Holy of Holies beyond. Prayer brings us to the very gates of heaven. When we are at the mercy-seat, we are partly on earth, and partly in heaven. Our prayers are there already and we are breathing the very breath of heaven. It is all open; it is one blessed chamber where we have fellowship not only with our brethren below, but with the hearts that wait for us above. So it was that while Jesus was praying He was transfigured before them. And so it was that while Stephen was praying, his face

became like the face of an angel. And
so it is that while you wait upon your
Lord you shall change your strength;
"you shall mount up with wings as
eagles; run and not be weary; walk and
not faint."

The effects of this incense and of this
altar were very beautiful. We have a
description of them in the eighth chapter of Revelation, where we read of the
angel that came down and gathered up
the prayers of the saints upon the golden
altar that was before the throne. And
then we read of a mighty angel (I am
quoting from two passages); there
was given him much incense that he
should offer it with the prayers of the
saints upon the altar before the throne.
It is an old interpretation that I do not
care to dispute, that this angel was the
Lord Jesus, that the incense was the
prayers of the saints and His intercessions mingled with the prayers of the
saints. And the meaning is that when
you send up your prayers before God,
although you may feel there is much that
is unworthy in them, yet the hands of the

blessed angel take them before they get to God. And I believe He drops from them every grain of impurity and only keeps that which is acceptable to the Father; and with that He mingles His own intercession, breathes His own breath upon your purified petitions, and with His holy hands, offers them at His Father's feet, until there comes the sweet answer of His love, and we are accepted in the Beloved. Beloved, what is all this to you?

There is an awful contrast here between the true fire and the false fire that some of the priests presumed to bring to God, and we know the consequence was most fearful vengeance. Anybody that should counterfeit this perfume should be cut off. To counterfeit was death; to counterfeit is death still. May I ask you, are you approaching the most holy Presence through the blood of Jesus? Or are you coming with your own natural thoughts, self-righteousness, and self-will? If you are doing the latter, you are bringing strange fire, and it will be death. Are you counterfeiting God's holy incense? Are you making feeling or sentiment, delightful music, or sacred eloquence or poetic rapture, or anything but the Spirit of God take the place of true devotion? Oh, if it is not in the name of Jesus, it is strange fire! It is counterfeit, and it is death. Or is anybody using the ministry of God to tickle the fancy of an audience, using this sacred desk to play with people's sentiments, using sacred song and holy worship and the very Church of God just to entertain or amuse the æsthetic tastes of people, even using God's incense for man's mercenary purposes? It is the counterfeiting of which He said of of old, "it is death."

Are you coming to God through any other means than Christ alone? Are you looking for salvation in any other way than through His death? "There is no other name given among men whereby we must be saved." Are you living this life of communion with God? Do you know this heavenly way? Have you ever experienced these divine communings? Is this figure of frankincense anything

to you? Is your heart anything like this
sweet place? Or is it a place of rank
and unclean things with the smell of
earthly carrion, and the unclean sewer-
age of your own sins? Oh, come to Him
to cleanse you, and in the place where
the dragons crawl, and where serpents
find their slimy haunts, He will dwell,
and the wilderness and the solitary place
shall blossom as the rose! And your
poor heart shall become like the very
gates of heaven, where angels will love
to gather, where the Dove of peace will
fold His wings and rest, and where you
shall say even in the darkest hour, "This
is none other than the house of God; this
is the gate of heaven." Beloved, have
you this little perfumed sanctuary? "1
will be to them a little sanctuary," says
God.

Some of us, as we walk through this
wilderness, are so sweetly conscious that
we are carrying our tent along, and it
folds around us every hot midday, and
every dark night the lamps are lighted
within, and the air is all sweet with the
very breath of heaven. "Blessed is the

man that Thou choosest and causest to
dwell in Thy presence." Beloved, come
and walk in the light of the Lord until
He shall say, "Come, ye blessed of My
Father, enter now," not the shifting tents
of the wilderness, but the palace of the
King.

CHAPTER VII.

THE ARK AND THE HOLY OF HOLIES.

"And they shall make an ark *of* shittim wood: two cubits and a half *shall be* the length thereof, and a cubit and a half the breadth thereof, and a cubit and a half the height thereof. And thou shalt overlay it with pure gold, within and without shalt thou overlay it, and shalt make upon it a crown of gold round about. And thou shalt cast four rings of gold for it, and put *them* in the four corners thereof; and two rings *shall be* in one side of it, and two rings in the other side of it. And thou shalt make staves of shittim wood, and overlay them with gold. And thou shalt put the staves into the rings by the sides of the ark, that the ark may be borne with them. The staves shall be in the rings of the ark; they shall not be taken from it. And thou shalt put into the ark the testimony which I shall give the. And thou shalt make a mercy-seat of pure gold; two cubits and a half *shall be* the length thereof, and a cubit and a half the breadth thereof. And thou shalt make two cherubims *of* gold, *of* beaten work thou shalt make them, in the two ends of the mercy-seat. And make one cherub on the one end, and the other cherub on the other end; even of the mercy-seat shall ye make the cherubims on the two ends thereof. And the cherubims shall stretch forth *their* wings on high, covering the mercy-seat with their wings, and their faces *shall look* one to another; toward the mercy-seat shall the faces of the cherubims be. And thou shalt put the mercy-seat above upon the ark; and in the ark thou shalt put the testimony that I shall give thee. And there I will meet with thee, and I will commune with thee from above the mercy-seat, from between the two cherubims which are upon the ark of the testimony, of all *things* which I will give thee in commandment unto the children of Israel.'' Ex. 25: 10-22.

''There was a tabernacle made; the first, wherein was the candlestick, and the table and the shewbread; which is called the sanctuary. And after the second vail, the tabernacle, which is called the Holiest of all; which had the golden censer, and the ark of the covenant overlaid round about with gold, wherein *was* the golden pot that had manna, and Aaron's rod that budded, and the tables of the covenant; and over it the cherubims of glory shadowing the mercy-seat: of which we cannot now speak particularly.''—Heb. 9: 2-5.

WE need not dwell on the form and dimensions of this remaining portion of the Tabernacle. You will understand, I think, that the inner chamber was a perfect cube, separated from the outer sanctuary by the costly and gorgeous curtain called the vail, and containing the most beautiful workmanship of any part of the structure, being wholly lined with gold, and adorned with the most elaborate embroideries. It contained a single article of furniture, a little chest called the ark, between two and three feet high, and over three feet long, and having within it the two tables of the law; and for a time, two other articles, of typical interest—the pot of manna preserved from the desert, and the rod of Aaron which had been the budding symbol of his divine and authoritative priesthood. The ark had also staves by which it was carried, through rings. Above it was the propitiatory, or mercy-seat, of solid gold, stained by the blood which was brought in by the high priest once a year. And above this mercy-seat rose the winged figures of the cherubim, meeting above it, while between their wings was constantly seen the shining forth of the presence of God, called the Shekinah, which ever hung there, and seems to have spread out into the cloud which guided them and sheltered them in their wilderness journey.

This chamber was the principal point of interest in the Tabernacle. It was the presence chamber of God. It was visited only once a year by the high priest, on the Day of Atonement, who carried the names of the people on his breast and shoulders and made reconciliation for

9

their sins. This has come to represent
the highest and deepest communion of
the soul with God. This inner chamber
is the secret place of the Most High,
where we can now enter in through the
blood of Jesus, opened to all since the
Saviour's death, and shedding its light
and glory on all our lives. It is yet more
emphatically a worthy and glorious type
of that which is still unrevealed, the
glory of the eternal world. It is a type
of the light which is inaccessible, the very
light of His presence who is Himself the
glory of the city that has no need of the
sun, but the Lamb is the light thereof.

1. The first lesson is connected with
the vail which once separated that sacred
chamber from it, but which has been
withdrawn and no longer secludes it.
This vail represents the obstructions
which came between the soul and God in
the Hebrew dispensation and obscured
the full revelation of His presence and
grace. And it represents, on the other
hand, the removal of these obstructions,
and the revelation which has since come
through the finished work of Christ. So

it stands, on the one hand, for separation, and the other for revelation, representing the things which once kept us from God, and then representing their removal and the way in which we may come to God in the most intimate fellowship. We are told that this vail was the flesh of Jesus Christ and that when His flesh was put aside by the Cross, this vail was rent in twain, and the Holy of Holies was opened to the view, and to the entrance of His believing and trusting people. Now, I cannot but believe that this was typical also of the entire fleshly life of the people of God and that the death of the Lord Jesus Christ is typical of the death into which we enter when we consecrate ourselves to God. And the removal of the vail, which was withdrawn through His death, represents the death which comes to us when we die with Christ, and rise into newness of life. As long, dear friends, as your flesh is indulged and suffered to remain, there is no way for you into the Holiest of all. You cannot see it. The old nature hinders our seeing the glory of God.

But when self dies, the vail is rent in twain, the glory of God opened, and the voice of the Spirit says: "Having therefore boldness to enter into the holiest by the blood of Jesus, by a new and living way, which he has consecrated for us, through the vail, that is to say, his flesh, let us draw near with a true heart, in full assurance of faith." Everything, therefore, that helps you to die to self, helps you to live in Him, and is the opening up of the glory of God to you. If you can say, "I am dead with Christ," and, "I am risen with Christ," I am sure you can understand something of the apostle's language in the same series of epistles: "That Christ may dwell in your heart by faith; that you may know the heights and depths of the love of Christ, which passeth knowledge, and be filled with all the fullness of God."

Beloved, has the vail been rent in twain for you by the death of self? If so, your heart is a holy Tabernacle, and there is no barrier there between you and the throne of God.

2. Let us step in reverently, and next

look at the mercy-seat. This is the golden lid of the ark of the covenant. The lid is the mercy-seat. It is the same gold that was wrought into the cherubim above. They are all of one piece. Now this literally means in Hebrew a bloody covering and the interpretation is that it hides something; it covers something that otherwise would be unfit to see. What did this mercy-seat cover? Imagine that this desk is the ark, and this lid is the mercy-seat. Imagine that the record of your sins is in this casket, that the broken law is there, the law, every line of which calls to heaven against you, every line of which is a witness of your sin. You have broken it; there is appealing to God for judgment. And imagine that there is no lid on the ark, that it is all open: and that your sin is recorded on the stony table and witnessing against you forever. And now, see above you the awful Shekinah eye, looking on the record. Now suppose that your sin was there, and God was looking down; would you not want something to come between and hide it from His sight?

And if you saw an angel's hand bring
a lid of pure gold, imperishable, something that could not be broken nor removed, and shut it down over the record
of sin, and with the other hand come and
sprinkle the blood which answered back
heaven for your sin, and which said to
that holy eye, "Punished, pardoned, ran-
somed,—laid on me,—Father, forgive
them," would not that be a glorious covering?   That is just what it is, and
so David sings, "Blessed is the man
whose iniquity is forgiven; whose sin is
covered."   It is the same word used
for mercy-seat. And again we read, "He
hath not seen iniquity in Jacob, or per-
verseness in Israel."   Why? Because
it was covered.   O, beloved, this is the
meaning of salvation—covered forever
by the blood of Jesus, by the righteousness of Jesus!

And so this mercy-seat has come to
represent God's mercy. But further, it
has come to mean the privilege of communion and of fellowship, on the ground
of Christ's atonement and intercession.

The Lord says, "There will I meet with

thee, and I will commune with thee from between the cherubim." There is nothing between now, no guilt, no sin, no fear. You can bring your desires and your needs, and you can come again and again, for there is no vail now. The vail is put aside, and the voice of love is saying, "Let us draw near with full assurance of faith," and "Let us come boldly unto the throne of grace, that we may obtain mercy and find grace to help in time of need." O, beloved, do you know all the blessed meaning of the mercy-seat?

Our hearts may well throb with loving notes of praise, as we think of all this means. "I love the Lord because he hath heard the voice of my supplications; therefore will I call upon him as long as I live."

3. Now let us look at the ark. It is the special type of Christ; He is the sacrifice, and the glory and the very centre of salvation and of reconciliation with God. The highest meaning of this ancient Tabernacle is, the everlasting Gospel. So this ark, and everything

about the ark, were types of Christ and salvation. The mercy-seat was the lid of the ark, and the cherubim were the expansion of the mercy-seat. So it means that Jesus Christ is the first and the last, the substance, the Alpha and Omega of that glorious world of which this was the picture. There is nothing there but the ark and its accompaniments. And if we get to heaven we shall see only Jesus. If you look at the Father, you will see Jesus as the fullness of His glory, The angels wait on Him. There is nothing in heaven but Jesus, and there ought to be nothing on earth. We ought to be able to say, "Jesus, the fairest among ten thousand, the one altogether lovely. There is none that I desire beside Him." And Jesus fills up all the heart if you will let Him. He is big enough for the altar of sacrifice, big enough for the Holy of Holies, big enough for your little heart.

Then this glorious ark was the leader of the people; it was the constant pledge of guidance and victory; wherever they went before them. There was a short

time when Moses got a little anxious,
and he said to his brother-in-law, Hobab,
"You are a wise old sheik, I wish you
would stay with us and show us the
way," God did not say anything then,
but the next morning He a gave a new
commandment. He said, "Take the ark
and carry it out in front of the host,
and it shall lead them." So Moses saw
that it was to be the guide, "to search
out a resting place for them," So,
again, when they came to Jordan's
stormy tide, and swollen waters flowed
between them and the promised land,
as that ark entered the waters, they were
swept aside and Israel went forward in
triumph. It stands for Jesus, our mighty
Leader, the Captain of our salvation.
When we come to the swollen tides of
trouble, He will carry us through; and
when the river overflows its banks in
the Jordan of death, they, too, shall roll
asunder, and He shall lead on, the mighty
conqueror of death. "If a man keep my
commandments he will never see death."
He will say: "Where is death? I cannot
see it, I cannot see even the traces of

the river; there is nothing here but
Jesus; there is nothing here but the
gates of heaven; death is all gone.''

And, again, that ark contained His perfect righteousness. We read that there
were three things in the ark: First, the
table of the covenant; second, the rod
of Aaron that budded; thirdly, the pot
of manna taken from the wilderness as
a memorial. The first of these teaches
us that Jesus Christ, our ark, had in
His very heart, and as His very nature,
the perfect righteousness of God. The
divine law was enshrined in His bosom,
and so perfectly kept that He brought
in a perfect righteousness. He is the
only one that has kept or can keep God's
perfect law. You remember that the
first table was broken, the type, I believe, of the fact that when God gave the
law to Adam, he broke it; but the second
time He gave the law to Moses it was
kept in the ark. So, under the new dispensation, Jesus came down and kept
the law. Though it has been the witness
of our sin, yet He has fulfilled it.

This is an old story, but it will be

told as long as men live, and it will ever be new to some. So I tell it again today, the only way in which any man can be saved is by getting Christ's righteousness. This is your justification.

But there is another thought greater than this, and I hope it will not be a hard thing for any of you to understand. It is not enough for Jesus Christ to keep the law for you, but Jesus Christ wants to come into our hearts and keep the law *in* you. And so, not only was the law in the ark, but the ark was in the sanctuary. If you are the dwelling place of the Holy Spirit, in the very centre of your soul Jesus in enshrined, as the ark was in the Tabernacle. But in the very heart of the ark the law was enshrined; and so the very holiness of Jesus will be enshrined in you, if He is in you. Open your heart, beloved, and let Christ come in, and bring His righteousness and holiness. If Christ is in you, His holiness is in you, and He keeps everything. This is the secret of divine holiness—Christ in the heart our life and righteousness.

There was another thing in the ark— the rod that budded. This was the picture of Aaron's priesthood, and the buds represent its freshness. It was always new. It represents Jesus at God's right hand praying for us. And the buds on the rod suggest the freshness of Christ's intercessions. Every morning there is something new. O, my friend, in your heart this morning there are roses that never bloomed before; there are lilies whose sweet fragrance never breathed until this morning; there are little dewdrops just come to refresh your soul! Here are the fresh blossoms of peace and joy and healing. "In the beauty of holiness, from the womb of the morning: thou hast the dew of thy youth." Have you been breathing these flowers? Then there is nothing unclean in your heart. Have you been bathing in these dewdrops? Then everything is fresh with you this morning.

The pot of manna means His constant provision, heavenly bread ever kept for you. There may be no bread on your

table before you, but there is bread inside.

It was very remarkable that when this
ark was taken to the temple of Solomon,
two of the things were taken out, and
only one remained. In the wilderness it
had the three, but when it was removed
to the top of Mount Moriah, the pot of
manna and the rod were taken out, and
nothing was left but the law. I think that
this means that, when we get home, we
shall not want any more manna; nor shall
we have the buds, they will all have become the glorious fruits of paradise. Instead of the dewdrops and the flowers
and the promises of fruits, we shall have
the tree that yields her fruit every month.

4. Again, the cherubim, which over-
shadowed the mercy-seat with their four
faces—the lion, the ox, the man and the
eagle, represented the human-hearted-
ness of the man, the strength of the ox,
the majesty of the lion, the flight of the
eagle, as attributes of Jesus Christ, and
yet to belong to His brethren. It was
the picture of the glory of the redeemed
to which we are marching on. By and

by you will be as kingly as Jesus, you
will be as strong as Jesus, and you
will be as lofty as Jesus, and you
will be as spotless as the Son of Man is
today. God put the picture there
that we might see it, just as if you
could take your baby boy and hold up
the picture of his manhood, perhaps a
king upon the throne, and say, ''Now,
darling, keep your eye on that, and let
it keep you from everything low and
mean; always keep in your mind that
that is to be your future destiny.''

5. Finally, through the wings of these
glorious cherubim shone the light of the
Shekinah, the presence of God Himself.
That is the best of all. That is the
light which shall no more go down. That
is the sun which shall no more withdraw
its shining, but thy God shall be thy everlasting light. And bye and bye it shall
be brighter than ten thousand suns; and
even in its reflected glory, the righteous
shall shine forth as the sun in the Kingdom of their Father.

In conclusion: First, live in the inner
chamber; the door is open all the time;

and let your earthly life be in heaven,
and in the fullness of heaven's grace and
glory; secondly, keep your hopes high.
There is something better yet; keep your
eye upon it and where your treasure is,
there will your heart be, too.